CONFIDENCE

CONFIDENCE

HOW TO SUCCEED AT BEING YOURSELF

ALAN LOY McGINNIS

AUGSBURG Publishing House

CONFIDENCE
How to Succeed at Being Yourself

Copyright © 1987 Augsburg Publishing House

Library of Congress Cataloging-in-Publication Data

McGinnis, Alan Loy.
  CONFIDENCE: how to succeed at being yourself.

  Bibliography: p.
  Includes index.
  1. Self-confidence.   2. Self-perception.   I. Title.
BF575.S39M37   1987   158'.1   87-1470
ISBN 0-8066-2261-X
ISBN 0-8066-2262-8 (pbk.)

Manufactured in the U.S.A.   APH 10-1639

1 2 3 4 5 6 7 8 9 0 1 2 3 4 5 6 7 8 9

Dedication

This book is dedicated to Taz W. Kinney, M.D., who has been my partner for nearly 15 years. When we began together he was a board-certified psychiatrist with many years' experience in medicine. I was merely a clergyman with minimal training as a family therapist. But he took me in as if I were his equal, became both a father and a friend, and freely shared with me everything he knew. Unlike so many physicians who seem to become prima donnas, my partner is as down-to-earth as the Kentucky roots from which he comes, and he is more like a country doctor than a psychiatrist.

Taz and I often duck into each other's offices for a quick word between sessions. Sometimes I am asking for his advice, sometimes we need to make each other laugh, sometimes we need to check with one another to be sure that we are doing all that can be done for some of our clients. I value those glancing contacts with him because his insight is so fresh. He has never allowed himself to become cynical and jaded, and he has an almost childlike faith.

Sitting in my office one day, he asked what I was going to write about next. I told him that it would be something about self-image, and that we were thinking of a one-word title: *Confidence*. He stared out the window for a moment, and then said, "You know, I've often thought that if I could be God for just a few seconds, the one thing I would grant to people would be the ability to feel better about themselves."

This book does not have all the answers on developing a sense of self-worth, but such as it is, it is for Taz W. Kinney.

Also by
Dr. Alan Loy McGinnis

Books

The Friendship Factor (Minneapolis: Augsburg, 1979)
The Romance Factor (San Francisco: Harper & Row, 1982)
Bringing Out the Best in People (Minneapolis: Augsburg, 1985)

Audiocassettes

How to Get Closer to the People You Care For (Audio talks by Dr. McGinnis based on the book *The Friendship Factor,* with additional new material.)

The Romance Factor (Audio talks by Dr. McGinnis based on the book *The Romance Factor,* a handbook on love and marriage.)

Motivation without Manipulation: Bringing Out the Best in People (Audio talks by Dr. McGinnis based on the book *Bringing Out the Best in People,* containing additional, new information not in print.)

Confidence: How to Succeed at Being Yourself (Audio talks by Dr. McGinnis on envisioning a confident self.)

Alan Loy McGinnis may be contacted at Valley Counseling Center, 517 E. Wilson Ave., Suite 204, Glendale, California 91206, (818) 240-9322.

Contents

PART FIVE: HOW LOVE LEADS TO SELF-CONFIDENCE

Twelve Rules
for Building
Self-Confidence

1. Focus on your potential instead of your limitations.
2. Determine to know the truth about yourself.
3. Distinguish between who you are and what you do.
4. Find something you like to do and do well, then do it over and over.
5. Replace self-criticism with regular, positive self-talk.
6. Replace fear of failure with clear pictures of yourself functioning successfully and happily.
7. Dare to be a little eccentric.
8. Make the best possible peace with your parents.
9. Determine to integrate the body and spirit.
10. Determine to live above neurotic guilt.
11. Cultivate people who help you grow.
12. Refuse to allow rejection to keep you from taking the initiative with people.

Author's Note

The following people have read this book in various incarnations and improved it with their suggestions: Cindy Adams, Dr. Dennis Denning, Pat and Jane Henry, Dr. Taz Kinney, Tricia Kinney, Dr. Lee Kliewer, David Leek, Norman Lobsenz, Alan McGinnis Jr., Sherie Newell, Dr. Walter Ray, Godfrey Smith III, Mike Somdal, Mary Alice Spangler, Dr. Robert Swinney, and Dr. John Todd. Dr. Neil Warren is the most cogent thinker I know on the topic this book addresses and I owe a great deal to our conversations. It would be imposing on our friendship, however, to hold him responsible for the ideas that follow. Susan Rivers has been an invaluable associate throughout this project. Finally, my thanks to the staff of Augsburg Publishing House. In particular, I wish to thank Roland Seboldt and Robert Moluf, who are editors *par excellence*.

Many of the stories in this book are drawn from the lives of clients with whom I work, but have been sufficiently scrambled so that these persons will not be recognizable, even by intimate friends. The outlines of their emotional lives, however, are accurate.

*There is no value-judgment more important
to man—no factor more decisive in his
psychological development and motivation—
than the estimate he passes on himself.*

—NATHANIEL BRANDEN

Self-Confidence and the Discovery of Joy

OUR SUCCESS AT FRIENDSHIP, business, sports, love—indeed, at nearly every enterprise we attempt—is largely determined by our self-image. People who have a confidence in their personal worth seem to be magnets for success and happiness. Good things drop into their laps regularly, their relationships are long-lasting, their projects are usually carried to completion, and they have a way of enjoying the pleasures that the day brings. To use Blake's phrase, they "catch joy on the wing."

On the other hand, some people seem to be magnets for failure and unhappiness. Their plans go awry, they have a way of torpedoing their own successes, and nothing seems to work out for them. In the counseling office where I work we see many such persons. In most instances my colleagues and I find that their problems stem from a difficulty with self-acceptance. And when we are able to help them gain more confidence, many of their psychological troubles take care of themselves.

Can Your Self-Image Be Changed?

One of the pleasures of doing counseling over a number of decades is that occasionally one sees former clients who have made remarkable improvements. A person with whom I had worked intensively many years ago, and who has been living in another city, dropped by my office recently. I vividly recall the slouched young woman she once was. As she had sat in front of me week after week she had blushed, stumbled in her speech, and looked at the floor. Her body language said, "I don't even deserve to be talking to you." She tended to lose jobs, her relationships usually went sour, and she was having trouble in almost every area of her life. As we worked together it became clear that these failures were connected to the standards by which she judged herself.

Now, almost 10 years later, her self-estimate has obviously changed, for she is a startlingly transformed woman. She is beautifully poised, and her body language telegraphs how good she feels about herself. She talks with animation about the successful business she has started, she is contentedly married to a man she loves, and she has several long-term friends.

Some writers express considerable gloom about the ability of human beings to change. Sigmund Freud certainly doubted that they could, and the accepted wisdom in certain quarters still is that one's personality is largely determined in childhood.

But the fact of the matter is that we *can* change our self-perception. Someone who has acquired a low self-image is not doomed to a life of unhappiness and un-earned guilt. It is possible, by using certain techniques, to rid yourself of many negative attitudes and gain a healthy confidence in yourself.

Consider this man, who had several strikes against him. As a boy he was extremely thin and painfully shy. He wanted to be hard-boiled, tough, and fat, but no matter how many milk shakes and banana splits he downed, he couldn't gain a pound. To make matters worse, he was a minister's son, and that was an in-hibiting factor for somebody growing up in the small towns of Ohio. Practically every member of his family was a performer in public—a platform speaker—and that was the last thing he wanted to be.

"I was shy and bashful," he says, "and this self-image of inadequacy might have gone on indefinitely had it not been for something a professor said to me during my sophomore year in college. One day after I had made a miserable showing, he told me to wait after class. 'How long are you going to be bashful like this, a scared rabbit afraid of the sound of your own voice?' he demanded. 'You'd better change the way you think about yourself, Peale, before it's too late.' "

That may sound like a strong dose of medicine for the young boy, but it worked. The boy's name was

Norman Vincent Peale, and he went on to become one of America's most popular preachers and writers.

You'd better change the way you think about yourself. Is it really possible to make such a change? After that encounter, Peale says, something *did* change: "The inferiority feelings were not all gone; I have some of them to this day. But I changed the *image* I had of myself—and with it the course of my life."

Self-Confidence without Self-Worship

Is it possible to have too much confidence? Yes, it is. We all run across people with big egos who make life miserable for everyone. Unfortunately, when we think of confidence we often think of cockiness, arrogance, and conceit; or worse, we think of the smug, overbearing attitude that slick operators have when they are in positions of power.

There is something pathetic about members of a weekend seminar—at least of the type that is endemic to southern California—in which participants stand in a room and shout over and over, "I like myself, I like myself, I like myself." With the enormous emphasis on introspection and "finding yourself" in current pop psychology, many people emerge from therapy self-focused, self-centered, and self-absorbed. One man, whose wife left him a few months ago, went to see a counselor. He says, "After some therapy I now know that Jan lost a wonderful man. I've recently fallen in love with a fantastic person—myself."

Such talk is a little hard to take, but once past the pathetic attempt at self-aggrandizement, one cannot help feeling sorry for this man. At the behest of some modern-day shaman, he has inflated his ego and become very self-centered. The tragedy is that his narcissism, if allowed to run amuck in this fashion, will soon alienate the very people whose love he needs during this crisis.

The apostle Paul urged that we not think of ourselves more highly than we ought to think. The question then becomes, Just how highly *ought* we think of ourselves? The answer lies somewhere between the self-worship advocated by the secular psychologists and the false modesty conveyed by some misguided Christians. As we investigate ways to enhance our self-confidence, we will in this book also explore the nature of Christian humility. For what is needed in our day is an understanding of that middle ground where one is neither a braggart nor a wimp.

Why Resolutions to Improve Ourselves Tend to Fail

Many of us are regularly putting ourselves on some new self-improvement program. We are determined to lose weight, stop smoking, start exercising, read faster, or begin aerobics. When most of us embark on such programs it is because we are unhappy with ourselves and think that if we can change some behavior, we will be happy.

The fallacy here is in assuming that if our exterior changes, we will feel better on the inside. There is enough truth in that assumption to lead us far astray. When we get awards and degrees, a good feeling *does* accompany the achievement, and we can jump to the conclusion that by changing things on the outside—by doing all the things that other people seem to want—our inner world will change.

But in fact it works the other way. Most change starts on the inside and works outward. It begins with self-knowledge and self-enrichment. It has to do with changing our thinking as well as our behavior; and if we can reform the way we think, if we can talk to ourselves and picture ourselves differently, then a great deal of our behavior will automatically fall into place.

The aim of this book is to provide strategies for changing that interior world. Here you will find simple, practical, time-tested techniques that thousands of successful people have used to convert self-doubt into self-confidence. Some are daily exercises to build up your self-image; others are principles to fall back on when your self-regard is too dependent on your successes and failures.

Reversing the way you think about yourself will not happen overnight, and it cannot happen without effort. But it *is* possible, and confidence is a commodity available to everyone. "Fears are educated into us," Dr. Karl Menninger once wrote, "and they can, if we wish, be educated out."

PART
. . . . . .
O N E

FOUR
FUNDAMENTALS
FOR DEVELOPING
SELF-CONFIDENCE

CONFIDENCE

· · · · · · · · ·

CHAPTER ONE

*I believe fervently in our species
and have no patience with the current fashion
of running down the human being
as a useful part of nature.
On the contrary, we are a spectacular, splendid
manifestation of life.*

—LEWIS THOMAS, M.D.

Tapping
Your Capacities

WHEN HELEN HAYES was a young actress, her producer, George Tyler, told her that, were she four inches taller, she could become one of the great actresses of her time. "I decided," she says, "to lick my size. A string of teachers pulled and stretched till I felt I was in a medieval torture chamber. I gained nary an inch—but my posture became military. I became the tallest five-foot woman in the world. And my refusal to be limited by my limitations enabled me to play Mary of Scotland, one of the tallest queens in history."

Helen Hayes succeeded because she refused to focus on her weaknesses, but rather chose to focus on her strong points and on her potential. And that is the first fundamental for developing confidence:

FOCUS ON YOUR POTENTIAL INSTEAD OF YOUR LIMITATIONS

In this book I do not want to give the kind of Pollyanna advice or promote the sort of irresponsible notions that one hears from many motivational speakers. They tell us that we are wonderful, that our possibilities are limitless, and that if we will simply believe in ourselves we can accomplish anything. We are *not* wonderful in every way, we do not operate without certain limitations, and merely believing ourselves omnipotent will not make ourselves so. When we tell our children that they can accomplish anything they want, we sometimes crush their self-confidence rather than increase it, because when their dreams do not come true, they assume that there is something wrong with them. It is cruel to tell a tone-deaf girl that she can become a great soprano, or a boy with a below-average IQ that he can become a doctor.

But it is not unrealistic to tell our children that they are created by God and therefore very important, that within them lie untapped and powerful resources, that they are far more *potentially* than they are *actually*. The positive thinkers are for the most part right: we *do* carry within us the possibility of changing the world by changing our attitudes, and they are correct to speak of the incredible potential of the human organism. In the last book he wrote, Einstein decried the fact that only a small portion of his capacities had been tapped. And Admiral Byrd, who was the first person to fly over the North and South Poles, said, "Few people come anywhere near exhausting the resources within them. There are deep wells of strength that are never used."

The Concept of Creation

Many of my clients tell me that they are not as smart or good-looking or witty as others and that they feel inferior. These people, incidentally, are not mentally ill. There was a time when you went to a psychiatric clinic only when you were suicidally depressed or hearing voices. But today our waiting rooms are filled with normal, functioning people who are simply unhappy.

I wish I could say to clients who feel inadequate and inferior, "Oh, come now, you are as smart as anyone," but in some cases it would be dishonest. Despite what the *Declaration of Independence* says, we are *not* all created equal. So instead I try to help them realize that they have been magnificently created by a great God, and for *that* reason they matter. We begin building self-confidence when we believe that we originated from a benevolent Creator.

Standing on the windswept shores of Lake Michigan one wintry night, ready to throw himself into the freezing waters, a 32-year-old bankrupt dropout happened to gaze up at the starry heavens. Suddenly, he felt a rush of awe, and a thought flashed through his mind: *You have no right to eliminate yourself. You do not belong to you. You belong to the universe.* R. Buck-minster Fuller turned his back to the lake and began a remarkable career. Best-known as the inventor of the geodesic dome, by the time of his death he held more than 170 patents and was world-famous as an engineer, mathematician, architect, and poet.

Buckminster Fuller's experience that night on Lake Michigan merely echoed the words of the ancient psalmist, who also contemplated the night sky and was awed by its grandeur:

> When I consider your heavens,
> the work of your fingers,
> the moon and the stars,
> which you have set in place,
> what is man that you are mindful of him,
> the son of man that you care for him?

The psalmist was inclined to feel insecure and inad-equate in the face of such magnificence, but back came a resounding reply to his question:

> You made him a little lower than God
> and crowned him with glory and honor (Ps. 8:3-5).

Like it or not (for it does carry with it certain respon-sibilities as well as glories), we have been created by God, and our Creator has endowed us with remarkable capacities.

The Internal Filter

But if God has really created human beings with such glory and honor, what keeps so many of us from tapping our potential? Frequently it is because we get obsessed with our defects rather than looking at the whole picture. A pretty girl is preparing to go out on a date. It happens that she has a pimple on her chin this week. Does she see all the good qualities that would cause most objective observers (such as her date) to look at her and say that she is beautiful? No, she sees only the pimple. And if the boy she goes out with tries to compliment her, she is likely to take it as mere flattery, or worse, as a lie.

One of the strangest things we observe in therapy is that people who doubt themselves often cannot accept compliments. One would suppose that if people have low self-confidence, they would be eager to accept accolades. But it is the opposite: if their self-perception is off and they dislike the way they are, they will not be talked out of that self-view, no matter what people try to say. When someone criticizes, they hear every word, but compliments drift over them.

Here is the way it works. We appear to have an inner filter that allows only certain data in. That is, you hear only the remarks that conform to your view of yourself. Let's say you believe the following things about yourself:

- I'm pretty good at sports.
- I'm poor at math.
- My IQ is about average.
- I've got a pretty face but a terrible figure.

When new data comes toward you, it is run through this filter. If it fits what you think you are, then the filter lets it in. If someone says, "You're really good at tennis," that's allowed in, and you thank the person for the compliment, because the remark conforms to your belief system (I'm good at sports). But if someone says, "You're sure looking nice and trim," that is screened out, because your inner picture is of someone with a terrible figure.

A few years ago I saw a dramatic instance of such skewed self-perception in one of our therapy groups. We were going around the room talking about body images, and when we got to one woman, she said, "Well, I see myself as fat and pimply." At that, the group broke into laughter, because she was about 5'8" and slender as a model, with beautiful, long hair and clear skin. What had happened was that in adolescence she *had* been fat and pimply. People had let her know how unattractive she was—probably with great cruelty. This internal picture of herself did not change when she changed. Hadn't anyone been telling her in the meantime that she was beautiful and slender? I'm fairly certain they had. But her filter had successfully screened those compliments out.

Getting away from Comparisons

There is another factor that causes us to be obsessed with our limitations: the tendency to compare ourselves with others. There is probably no other habit that chips away at our self-confidence so effectively as the habit of scanning the people around us to see how we compare. It is as if we have a radar dish on our foreheads, constantly searching to see if someone else is quicker, tanner, or brighter. And when we find that at times someone is, we are devastated.

FOUR FUNDAMENTALS FOR SELF-CONFIDENCE
■

The folly of basing our self-estimate on comparisons is that it puts us on a roller-coaster. Perhaps we are feeling fairly good about our appearance one day, and we find ourselves in the company of someone with stunningly good looks. Suddenly we feel ugly and want to disappear. Or perhaps we *know* we have above-average intelligence, but we happen to be at lunch with people who are even smarter. Then every word that comes out of our mouths sounds like intellectual sludge.

Some of us grew up with older brothers and sisters who we desperately wanted to emulate, but of course we were doomed from the start. For no matter how hard we tried to catch up, we found ourselves smaller, clumsier, and dumber than they were. And when they ridiculed us—as all older siblings do—we learned to criticize ourselves. In many cases this became a life-long habit.

But God did not make us to be like our siblings or anyone else. We are absolutely unique. We are the product of 23 chromosomes from our mothers and 23 chromosomes from our fathers, and geneticists say that the odds of our parents having another child like us are one in $10^{2,000,000,000}$. The combination of attributes that constitutes us will never be duplicated. If this is true, and if it is true that we are created by God—an original by a master artist—it makes the exploration and development of that uniqueness an item of the highest priority.

Our core value is not diminished when we happen to be with people who are better musicians or more famous or wealthier. Nor is it heightened when we find ourselves with people who are less accomplished. The

Bible teaches that we have worth quite apart from the existence of any other person. We have worth because we are God's unique creation.

The Hasidic rabbi, Zuscha, was asked on his deathbed what he thought the kingdom of God would be like. He replied, "I don't know. But one thing I do know. When I get there I am not going to be asked, 'Why weren't you Moses? Why weren't you David?' I am only going to be asked, 'Why weren't you Zuscha? Why weren't you fully you?' "

Thousands of years ago, the Greek philosopher Aristotle suggested that each human being is bred with a unique set of potentials that yearn to be fulfilled as surely as the acorn yearns to become the oak within it. Sidney Poitier's parents probably never heard of Aristotle's notion, but they knew its truth in their bones and they taught their children a self-reliance that refused to be defeated because they had some limitations.

"I was a product of a colonial system," says Poitier, "that was very damaging to the psyche of non-white people. The darker you were, the less opportunities were presented to you. . . . My parents were terribly, terribly poor, and after a while the psychology of poverty begins to mess with your head. As a result, I cultivated a fierce pride in myself, something that was hammered into me by my parents Evelyn and Reggie— mostly by Evelyn. She never apologized for the fact that she had to make my pants out of flour sacks. I used to have 'Imperial Flour' written across my rear. She always used to say 'If it's clean, that's the important thing.' So from that woman—and probably for that woman—I always wanted to be extraordinary."

Doing the Best You Can
with What You've Got

All of us have weaknesses. The trick is to determine which ones are improvable, then get to work on those and forget about the rest. For example, some of us will never be as good at math as others. But the important thing is to stop kicking ourselves when we are not quick at math problems and develop the things we *are* good at. Jesus' parable about the talents has as its inescapable conclusion that the distribution of gifts in this world is not our concern. Our responsibility is to take the talents with which we find ourselves and ardently parlay them to the highest possible achievement.

Take the case of Yoshihiko Yamamoto, of Nagoya City, Japan. When he was six months old his parents learned that he suffered from hydrocephalus, an abnormal accumulation of fluid on the brain. Physicians told his parents that their child was probably mentally retarded. With a hearing loss that strangled his speech and an IQ that was never tested at higher than 47, one would have thought his future very bleak.

But then he acquired a new special education teacher. Takashi Kawasaki liked his new, well-behaved pupil. Gradually the boy began to smile in class, and slowly he learned to copy the letters from the chalkboard and write his name. He spent long hours painstakingly copying cartoons from books and magazines.

One day Yamamoto drew an accurate sketch of the Nagoya Castle. The clear lines of the picture reminded his teacher of a print. He had the boy transfer his design to a wood block and encouraged him to concentrate on printmaking. Eventually, Kawasaki entered some of Yamamoto's prints in an art contest in Nagoya City, and he won first prize. Today bankers and storekeepers buy the student's work to adorn their walls. Yamamoto still requires a very ordered life and likes his schedule unvaried. He gets up at 7:00 every morning, makes his bed, eats breakfast at 7:40, and takes the 8:00 bus to school, where he writes in his picture diary and then works on his prints. At noon he goes to the shopping center, buys his favorite bread for lunch, and is back to school and at his prints promptly at 1:00. He leaves for home at 5:00, has supper, watches TV, and goes to bed on schedule.

Is it important that Yoshihiko Yamamoto does not have as high an IQ as most, or that he has limitations? No, the important thing is that he is doing the best he can with what he has. Rather than getting obsessed with his limitations, he has capitalized on his potential.

CONFIDENCE
• • • • • • • • •
CHAPTER TWO

. . . you will know the truth
and the truth will set you free.

—JOHN 8:32

Discovering
Your Inner Self

CAN YOU CURE LONELINESS?" Charlie Brown asked his nemesis, Lucy, who was lounging behind her booth that said, "Psychiatrist, 5¢."

"I can cure anything," she assured him.

"Can you cure deep-down, bottom-of-the-well, black-forever loneliness?"

"All for the same nickel?" she asked.

Some of us in the counseling business feel a little like Lucy at times. Our clients have deep-seated and long-standing problems, and simple answers will not suffice.

It is far too simple, for instance, to advise people who lack confidence that they should "love themselves." For one thing, most of us have things about us that we cannot love, things we want to change. In the second place, advising people to love themselves presumes that they know their inner beings, and *that* is a dangerous presumption. Freud proved without question that much of our behavior is motivated by unconscious mechanisms, and that we are remarkably ignorant of much of what drives us from within. Self-knowledge, then, is an essential part of self-confidence.

My clients often come expecting advice, but I try to make it clear that I am there more as a mirror than an advice giver. I tell people that the most important thing they can take away from our sessions is not what they hear me say but what they hear themselves saying. In the telling of their tale, they can make some remarkable discoveries about themselves. And that is no mean achievement, for to acquire self-understanding is to be well on the way to discovering joy.

The second fundamental, then, for developing self-confidence is:

··································

DETERMINE TO KNOW THE TRUTH ABOUT YOURSELF

··································

When starting therapy with new clients I often inquire what it would take for them to be happy. I sometimes ask it this way: "If you had unlimited money and could live whatever sort of life you'd enjoy, what would be the shape of your existence?" At first, most of them grin and talk of lying on some Caribbean beach and being on a permanent vacation. But they quickly agree that in a short time that would get boring. How, then, would they like to live? Often they are remarkably unable to go further with the question, which is to say that they are quite out of touch with their wishes, dreams, and preferences. They're unhappy and know they're unhappy, but they have lived so long by suppressing their emotions that the data is not readily accessible.

"I was never a beauty," said Golda Meir when she was prime minister of Israel. "There was a time when I was sorry about that, when I was old enough to understand the importance of it and, looking in the mirror, realized it was something I was never going to have."

How did Meir overcome those feelings of inferiority? "I found what I wanted to do in life," she writes, "and being called pretty no longer had any importance." She goes on to explain that in some ways *not* being beautiful was a blessing in disguise—it forced her to develop her inner resources. But the key doubtless lies in her remark, *"I found what I wanted to do in life."* Regrettably, many people with whom I work have lived so long out of contact with their deeper selves that they have no idea what they would like to do and be.

Why We Lose Contact with the Truth about Ourselves

How is it that we know ourselves so little, that we get so disconnected from our inner beings? Let's take a simple example, which I owe to Dr. Neil Warren. It is Saturday, and a three-year-old boy is playing on the sidewalk while his dad is washing the car in the driveway. Two older boys are playing across the street. He would never have the courage to go over and ask to play with them, but the boy wants to impress them, so he does some maneuvers with his wagon that result in his being dumped on the sidewalk. When he sees his skinned elbows, he begins to cry. Dad is a little embarrassed that his son was clumsy and now is crying so much that the older boys across the street are laughing. There is irritation in his voice as he says, "C'mon, stop your crying. You're not hurt that bad. Be a man."

The boy tries hard to sort out the confusion: *I feel like crying. I always cried before when I hurt. But crying makes daddy unhappy. Next time I'd better try not to cry.*

So the boy learns to bite his lip, to act as if his feelings are not there, and the process of denial begins. A little girl shows dislike for a relative or "hates" her brother, and mother tells her that such feelings are terrible. A child bursts into a room, full of enthusiasm and excitement, and is told by an irritated father, "Quiet down! What's wrong with you?" After hearing such messages hundreds of times, the child learns that to get along in the world you don't follow all your impulses and you often have to ignore your emotions.

Trying on Identities

A similar squelching can happen to us during adolescence, when most of us try on different personalities with the rapidity of changing outfits in a clothing store. If we happen to get caught experimenting with a bizarre identity, it can have strong repercussions.

A friend was waiting for a light at an intersection when a group of girls, most about age 13, crossed in front of his car. They were dressed in uniforms from one of the local prep schools. One girl yelled to him as she walked by, "Hi, handsome. Wanna party?" Then she giggled and ran to catch up with her friends, who were laughing as they watched from the curb. My friend thought she might have said it on a dare. Or more likely, she was merely experimenting with a totally different personality to see how it felt, and probably never tried that behavior again. Cynthia Heimel says, "The most distinguishing characteristic of a 14-year-old girl is that she has no distinguishing characteristic. They all say and think the same things. They make a frenzied dash toward individuality, then get scared and rush, shivering, back under Mommy's wing."

Ordinarily such experimentation is healthy, assuming parents understand that their children don't have a clear sense of identity. Heimel says, "Their personalities are still amorphous blobs. A 14-year-old may be dimly aware that she likes biology better than history, but that's about it. She is still molting."

But let's say that the parents of the girl who walked in front of my friend's car learn of her little antic from another parent and they are scandalized. That night they say to her: "We can't believe you did that. We had no idea what a terrible girl we have on our hands. What's happened to you?" And she had merely been trying on an identity that already had been discarded because it did not fit.

Very harsh parents can infect us with the notion that we have "terrible" thoughts and emotions, and thus fill us with terror of the inner life. We conclude that our feelings must be controlled, and, if possible, most should be eliminated. The result is that we learn to disown our feelings, which means that we cease to experience them.

A certain amount of emotional control is, of course, a necessary thing for children to learn. We cannot act like chimpanzees in society. But the process of socialization has some liabilities as well, for thus we learn to reject our inner selves.

Being Courageous about Our Imperfections

I am not saying that we are all innocent beauty within, if people would just let us express ourselves. It is a sign of health to be able to accept the negative aspects of ourselves, to look squarely at what Jung called "our shadow sides." The problem with some pop psychologies and Pollyanna religions is that they encourage people to embrace their gifts, celebrate themselves, and live positively, but do not provide any mechanism for confronting the evil that exists in us all.

The early church, on the other hand, was very realistic about human nature. "If we claim to be without sin, we deceive ourselves and the truth is not in us," the Bible says bluntly (1 John 1:8). This passage makes it clear that one of the steps on the way to wholeness is facing squarely the dark side of ourselves rather than sweeping it under the rug and proceeding as if it were not there.

Someone has said that the only emotion that can hurt us is the unacknowledged emotion. To repress our shadow side is to give it the greatest power over us.

Martin Buber said that good can be maximized not through the rejection or conquest of evil, but openly through the transformation of evil, the use of its energy and passion in the service of good. There is a catharsis and a liberation that comes from naming the thing we fear within.

Let's look at a simple illustration. When my clients are discussing a brother or sister who has succeeded more than they, I will often ask, "Are you jealous? Do you envy what your sister has?"

"Oh, no, I'm glad for her. She's my sister and I love her. No, I'm proud that she has accomplished so much."

But there is little conviction in the words, and it seems a stock response.

"Are you sure?" I may ask. "Wouldn't you like to succeed as much or more than she has? Don't you find that at times you resent her?"

There is a long look into my face to see if they can trust me, and to see if they really believe what they are about to say. Then out it comes:

"Well, maybe you're right. In fact, when the family gets together it galls me that everybody makes a fuss over her the way they do. I'm embarrassed to say it, because she's so good and she's worked hard for what she has, but yes, I'm jealous."

Self-Awareness vs. Self-Indulgence

To acknowledge the existence of certain desires and impulses does not mean that we are proud of them or that we plan to allow them free reign. To the contrary, we may say about some personality trait, or the memory of some shameful event from the past, "I don't *like* that it's there, and I intend to change some of this, but I acknowledge its existence." Such a step may seem rudimentary or even unnecessary to some, but in my work I have discovered that an enormous amount of denial goes on within us.

When I have urged certain clients to loosen the tight grip they keep on themselves in order to feel their pain and to embrace emotions such as anger or rejection, they frequently retort that it will do no good to feel sorry for themselves. But there is a difference between self-discovery and self-pity. Self-discovery is the opposite of self-pity, for it often requires great courage and honesty. Nathaniel Branden makes this distinction very clear:

> To be self-pitying is to make no effort to deal with one's suffering or to understand it, to complain of it while seeking to avoid confronting it, and to indulge in thoughts or utterances about the cruelty of life, the futility of struggle, the hopelessness of one's predicament. To say "Right now I am feeling hopeless" is not self-pity; to say "My situation is hopeless," is (usually) self-pity. In the first instance, one is describing a feeling; in the second, one is making a statement of alleged fact. Descriptions of feelings, however painful, can be therapeutic; statements of alleged facts about life or the world, motivated solely by one's painful emotions of the moment, generally are self-destructive. In the first case, one takes responsibility—the responsibility of awareness; in the second case, one abandons responsibility and surrenders to passivity.

Encounter with the Unconscious

If we are to know ourselves well we must explore our unconscious as well as our conscious self. Although I had done a great deal of counseling as a pastor, I did not enter therapy myself until I was in my thirties, and I was there only because outward circumstances had crumbled so badly that I had no choice. I went kicking and screaming, and once in, changed therapists several times. One doctor said, "McGinnis, you are more resistant to therapy than any patient I've ever treated." A psychiatrist proposed hypnosis, and I resisted that too. The prospect of giving up control to another person, and the possibility of discovering some perversions or some embarrassing experiences from the past, were very distasteful. But eventually I acquiesced.

Several months into the sessions, I thought, *This isn't working. He's not discovering any repressed traumas from childhood, or any shattering experiences that I've buried.* And indeed, nothing startling did turn up on those digs. At times, it didn't seem that I was in much of a trance, but a strange thing would happen. As I told the therapist about the images flitting across my mind, tears would begin to seep out from under my eyelids, and it was clear that we were in contact with a deeper self than I ordinarily knew.

It was not until a year after the therapy had ended that I began to realize what a great favor the therapist had done. He did not discover any keys to my immediate problems by probing with hypnosis—instead, he did something far more important: he helped me stop fearing my unconscious. I didn't like everything

38

we found there. But he helped me open a corridor between the conscious and the unconscious, and the two selves were no longer at such enmity. I stopped investing so much emotional energy in keeping material underground. Instead, I began to listen to that world, to tap into the deeper streams.

The Nature of the Unconscious

Freud, a confirmed atheist, steadfastly preached that the unconscious must be opened if we are to discover mental health and become better adjusted. But for him, taking the cover off the unconscious was something like taking the lid off a septic tank. Therein lay a dark and smelly world, dominated by aggressive tendencies and sexual aberrations.

C. G. Jung, on the other hand, was much more optimistic. He felt that if the unconscious has been tightly covered, one may indeed encounter a layer of dark material on the surface, but when that is skimmed away, the world of the unconscious is a beautiful place—the source of all creativity, including great art and music. In fact, Jung believed, it is largely in the unconscious that we meet God.

This optimistic view motivated Jung to plumb his own psyche, to attend carefully to the stirrings of that vast continent within. Jung paid careful attention to his dreams and never tired of peering into what he referred to as his "second self." This was true even when he was an old man. In 1959, after a very popular series of interviews on the BBC network, John Freeman asked him to write a book for lay readers. Jung demurred, saying that he was too old and that his writing career was over.

One night soon after that conversation he had a dream in which, instead of talking to Ph.D.s and physicians, he was standing in a public place and addressing a multitude of people who were listening with rapt attention and understanding what he said. Two weeks later he changed his mind and decided to write the book. The result was *Man and His Symbols*. When Jung finished his manuscript, it was as if his life's work was done. He died within months.

The Bible, of course, gives a great deal of credence to dreams, and in our discussion here we must remember that what is now called "the self" was once called "the soul," and that the exploration of the unconscious did not begin with Freud's publication of *The Interpretation of Dreams*. Jung, whose spiritual journey was a lifelong adventure, was close to the biblical thinkers and prophets in many ways. And he was willing to prod his unconscious relentlessly, to know the truth about himself.

Suggestions for Investigating Your Inner Self

I would like to emphasize that one does not necessarily require a therapist to engage in self-discovery. Freud and Jung analyzed themselves, and many of us can do the same. Here are some simple suggestions for learning more about your inner self.

1. Keep a journal. One help in self-analysis is the use of a personal journal. Dr. Gordon MacDonald, president of Inter-Varsity Christian Fellowship, talks about the importance of maintaining this spiritual discipline: "For many years I have kept a daily journal of what I am doing, why I am doing it, and what the results are. Just forcing it onto paper makes me ask what is going on in my life." That device will ensure a certain amount of objectivity, for when we look at our emotions and our lives on paper, it is easier to see our mistakes and the areas where we are deceiving ourselves.

Elizabeth O'Connor, whose books contain excellent material on the inward journey, makes these suggestions for journal keeping:

> Keep it for your own sake and your own eyes, so that you write in it without reservations. Let it be a description of your inner world and what is happening there. Put in it all the feelings you are aware of— feelings of love and hate and fear. Include what you unearth by your meditation. Write in it your prayers, your resolutions, the little dialogues you have with yourself, your dreams, your fantasies, your response to events and people. Let it be representative of both your spiritual and your psychological odyssey. . . . When you look back and read it, you will discover recurring themes and questions that will be helpful to consider further in times of meditation. Your journal is another way of being in dialogue with your many selves.

Remember, techniques such as this do not work for everyone, and if, after experimenting with a journal, it does not improve your self-knowledge, simply scrap the idea.

2. Arrange to spend time alone. Canadian pianist Glenn Gould believes that "for every hour that you spend in the company of other human beings you need X number of hours alone. Now what the X represents, I don't really know; it might be two and seven-eighths or seven and two-eighths, but it's a substantial ratio."

The lives of great persons in history have been checkered with solitude. Jesus, for all his interest in the poor and the needy, regularly retreated to replenish himself and to pray. Carl Sandburg once wrote of Lincoln: "In wilderness loneliness he companioned with trees, with weather and the changing season, with that individual and one-man instrument, the ax. In the making of him, the element of silence was immense."

We do our children a disservice if, when they complain of being bored, we quickly find an interesting program on television or drop what we are doing to entertain them. Those of us who grew up in the country before the days of television were very fortunate to learn early that one can get through to the other side of boredom. I recall long, hot days on the tractor, when steering was so tedious that it could be done without any thought. The only solution was to learn to daydream, and there on the tractor I first learned the power of spinning out detailed visions of what I wanted to be and have and do.

3. Note the things that make you distinctive. Rather than wasting mental energy strategizing how to be more like the crowd, you might do better to spend some of your thinking time on how you want to set yourself off from the herd. In your journal, for instance, it might be helpful to make a list from time to time under the heading, "How I Seem to Be Different." Write down the preferences and interests that make you unique.

Another way to implement this suggestion is to look back over your life and determine the times when you've been the happiest and most successful. In his book *What Color Is Your Parachute?* Richard Nelson Bolles reports that many people who are trying to decide on a career change have never taken inventory of their past experiences, listing in priority those accomplishments which made them happiest and most fulfilled. This is one more indication that most of us are acutely out of contact with our deeper selves. Recollections such as Bolles recommends can be a positive force, a guide calling us back to ourselves.

4. Regularly redefine yourself. I have been saying that we do well to try to get on paper who we are and where we are going. But we should be careful about any permanent definitions. It will not do to write up lists of distinctives, then put them aside, assuming that they will apply for the rest of our lives. As long as we live, we will be in a state of flux. The Tartar tribes of Central Asia had a curse they hurled against their enemies: "May you stay in one place forever." It is indeed a curse to remain the way we are forever. Life is not so much a matter of "finding" ourselves as it is a process of *making* ourselves.

A 36-year-old man once told me, "I've always regarded myself as shy, I suppose because my parents are that way. But now I'm beginning to wonder if that's who I am after all. I've been socializing more and more, and though I'm not the type to wear a lampshade at a party, I find that I enjoy talking and laughing with groups." I admired him as he spoke, for he was not allowing himself to calcify in a mold his parents had made. He was shifting, changing, and redefining himself as he went along.

5. *Look for someone in whom you can confide.* One of the remarkable things about Jesus was that he seemed to create a climate in which people felt free to talk and to share their innermost secrets. One of the values of such talk is that it helps us avoid self-delusion, for we human beings have an infinite capacity for self-deception. Having one other person who knows everything about us is enormously helpful in being able to see ourselves realistically.

Telling someone everything can help us learn a great deal about ourselves. The late Sidney Jourard went so far as to say that he could know himself *only* in the process of revealing himself to another: "I am beginning to suspect that I cannot even know my own soul except as I disclose it. I suspect that I will know myself 'for real' at the exact moment that I have succeeded in making it known through my disclosures to another person." That is probably an extreme statement, but there is no question that we learn about ourselves as we talk. I like it very much when a client says near the end of the hour, "Well, as I've been listening to myself talk I can see that. . . ."

Accurate self-knowledge is the first step in improving our self-image. We have been taught to deny so much, to put the best light on everything, to ignore the dark side of ourselves, and to eschew negative thinking. But facing the truth—especially the difficult truths about ourselves—can be both a liberating and an exhilarating experience. And the very decision to know the truth about ourselves is itself an act of self-acceptance.

*Watch a man at play for an hour
and you can learn more about him
than in talking to him for a year.*

—PLATO

Stepping Off
the Treadmill

I ONCE WENT TO A PARTY where the hostess had invited several people who did not know each other, and she put two restrictions on our conversations. In introducing ourselves we were not to tell: *(a)* our profession; or *(b)* whether or not we had children. It was revealing to see how uncomfortable we were in trying to make a connection with strangers without mentioning jobs and kids. There is no question about it: many of us define ourselves by what we do, and we try to position ourselves with others by the kinds of jobs we have, how much our children are achieving, and how well we've done financially. In other words, we are what we produce. This is a dangerous trap, for the result can be addiction to work and greed. So the third fundamental for developing self-confidence is:

DISTINGUISH BETWEEN WHO YOU ARE AND WHAT YOU DO

How did we confuse our personal value with our production so early on in life? We learned that it was not enough simply to *be* someone, but that we also had to *do* a great deal to be accepted.

A client of mine, who has been a stunning success in his business life but a failure in his personal life, tells about growing up in a home where work was the be-all and end-all of life. "My parents were the quintessential Puritan work ethic couple," he says. "They never went to parties and dinners, socialized very little, and put an enormous value on work.

"When my sister and I were young we didn't get a lot of strokes. Our parents weren't particularly affectionate. They loved us—no doubt about that. But they didn't hug us much and seemed worried that we would grow up with swollen heads, so modesty and humility were big virtues, and they didn't praise us much, either.

"But I knew that if I mowed the lawn especially well on Saturday, either dad would say to mom, or mom would say to dad at the dinner table: 'Tom did a good job on the lawn today, didn't he?' "

A child will do anything necessary to get strokes, so it is not difficult to guess how he worked at the lawn. Tom says, "I would mow the lawn across, then I'd go back and mow it up and down, then for good measure I'd go over it again on the angle. I would have done anything to get that little morsel of praise at dinner.

47

"When I was 11, my cousin let me help out in his machine shop, and during the summers I'd work every day, sweeping up shavings, running errands, painting. I was so hungry to work that I guess I was an ideal employee, even at 11. Dad would come home after talking to my cousin and tell mom how hard I'd been working at the shop, and I basked in the glory of it."

This young man found that his worth was tied to his production, so he naturally grew up working very, very hard. He always had a couple of jobs, and when he became an adult he was forever going to school, taking more classes, getting more degrees. But eventually it backfired. When he got married he assumed his wife would value him for the same reasons his mother had liked him. So he continued to lead the life of a hurried workaholic, taking it for granted that his wife would know that he was doing those things to please her. But it was a fatal mistake, for it turned out that she would rather have had him home watching TV, or simply sitting on the couch.

"With her I could simply *be*," he says. "She loved me pretty much as I was, without my scrambling to get another degree or setting another record for hours worked. I wish I had realized that sooner, because we might not be divorced now."

Your Self-Confidence and Your Net Worth

A related standard by which we judge ourselves is our net worth. The amount of money we have and the kind of car and house we own are often indicators of how successful we are at our careers, and these also have a powerful effect on the ever-changing barometer of our self-esteem. Why is it that we feel so much better about ourselves when we are driving a new car or when we invite friends over to see our new, luxurious townhouse? Or why is it that we do not like ourselves when people see us in a shabby car? It is because we think we have value for working hard and accumulating possessions.

The Superwoman

Many women today have set for themselves an impossible task: they think they should be able to juggle a career, children, and marriage, all with equal grace and aplomb. They may succeed at covering the bases, but many will naturally be better in one area than in another. A bright, articulate woman who makes a large income sat in my office recently and said, "I know I'm good at work, but when I close the door to the office and get on the freeway to go home, my self-confidence plummets. I'm not as good a cook as my husband, I get cranky with the baby, and I'm not a very good housekeeper. It's a wonder he hasn't left me by now." It turned out that her husband loved her a great deal and had no intention of leaving. He was proud of her success at work and his only real complaint about their life at home was that she couldn't relax and enjoy their evenings together.

Fortunately, some women who have spread themselves too thin are scaling down their self-expectations. But if they choose a career over children, they often have to make peace with biological and cultural stereotypes of the ideal female who does everything and does it all perfectly.

For other women, whose careers are their families, confusion arises when they tie their happiness to the success of their children. If the kids are doing well, they are fulfilled. But if one child does poorly in school or takes drugs or gets a divorce, they beat themselves with the question, "Where did I go wrong?" and sink into depression. As one woman said, "I can never be happier than my unhappiest child."

Such a close identification of our self-worth with our careers and children is a very slippery banana. Our careers are not always in our own hands. What happens to our self-confidence if the company we work for is sold and our entire department is abolished? And what happens when we do everything possible to be good parents and one of our children turns out to be an alcoholic? Finally, everyone must eventually retire and the nest must eventually empty, and unless we have some other foundation for our sense of worth, we are in trouble.

Production and Spirituality

The fundamental teaching from the Bible that illumines this topic is the doctrine of grace. It is normally related to the subject of redemption, but it has broader implications as well. The Bible is clear that God's love for us is not dependent on our work. That is, we are not loved by God because we scramble frenetically to read our Bibles, go to church, pray more, and avoid every sin possible. To the contrary, the love of God is a gift of grace, "not by works, so that no one can boast" (Eph. 2:9). In other words, God loves us simply and unconditionally because we are God's children. Dr. Lloyd John Ogilvie sums up the doctrine well when he says, "Nothing you could do could make God love you more than He does right now."

As St. Augustine made clear, the reality of God's grace does not mean that we are to sit down and become sinful slobs because our salvation is given to us rather than earned. To the contrary, when you feel in your bones the meaning of God's grace, you will want to lead a more godly life than ever. But the difference is this: you do it in response to God's love, rather than to earn that love. In the same fashion, when you feel valuable and loved by virtue of who you are rather than because of what you do, that does not make you want to spend the rest of your life lounging on the beach at Waikiki. Instead, this self-confidence causes you to want to accomplish all the more.

The Workaholic Syndrome

Those who have never discovered that God loves and accepts them tend to be driven, hurrying kinds of persons who are addicted to work. Two cardiologists, Meyer Friedman and Ray H. Rosenman, some years ago wrote a fascinating book entitled *Type A Behavior and Your Heart*. Their research on the correlation between personality type and coronary disease has since been superseded, but what they have to say about the psychology of the driven person is apt. Here, according to Friedman and Rosenman, are some signs that you are a workaholic, or Type A:

- If you usually feel vaguely guilty when you are relaxing and doing nothing for several hours or several days.
- When vacations are difficult.
- When you are always in a hurry, when you talk, eat and walk rapidly, and are constantly looking at your watch, worrying about being late.
- When you find yourself dropping into the conversation how late you worked last night, how early you arrived at the office this morning, or how many loads of wash you've done this week.
- If, upon meeting another driven person, you feel compelled to compete. This is a telltale trait because no one arouses the aggressive and/or hostile feelings of one Type A person more quickly than another Type A.
- If your frenzied, long-hour days cause you symptoms of stress, physical ailments such as headaches, ulcers, hypertension, and constant fatigue.
- If you quantify everything and find yourself evaluating not only your own but also the activities of others in terms of numbers—hours logged, time shortened, dollars earned.
- If you attempt to schedule more and more in less and less time and are unable to say no to people who want your services. This chronic sense of urgency and indispensability is one of the core components of the driven person.
- If you no longer observe interesting or lovely objects and are separated from the aesthetic and spiritual things that once gave you pleasure.

• If your relationships suffer because you are always too busy, too hurried, and put projects above people. (The divorce rate is markedly higher among people who fit the workaholic profile. The typical workaholic is often a man whose wife—if he still has one— says, "John has no real friends. I'm his only friend.")

Doing More but Accomplishing Less

The person who is addicted to work often is not nearly so effective as he or she would like to think. Many of the studies show that such persons do more but accomplish less. They give the appearance of turning out a blizzard of work, but in the long run they often do not accomplish as much as the less-driven person. High achievers are committed to results, whereas the driven person is simply committed to activity.

Driven workers have a way of flattening out in their careers. Dr. Charles Garfield says one can almost predict the professional trajectory of workaholics. They rise quickly on the basis of their initial contribution, and then they level off and end up managing the details of their careers instead of delegating those details to people they trust.

There is another sad thing about persons addicted to work as a way of establishing value: they can never meet their own standards. No matter how much they accomplish, it is never enough. These people are caught in a tragic bind: they can never feel of value when they are relaxing, and they can never do enough work to supply their need for confidence. When we are sitting, playing, watching TV, making love, or simply having fun, are we to assume that we are no good because we are not producing anything? It is an untenable position.

The Cure and Care of the Workaholic

Here are some guidelines (several of which are borrowed from Friedman and Rosenman) to help you shift the basis of your identity away from what you produce.

1. Engage in some honest self-appraisal of your work patterns. According to Friedman and Rosenman, four out of five Type A persons will deny that they are in that category or downplay the amount of driven behavior they display. You might want to ask your family and close friends to categorize you according to some of these standards. This will have a twofold benefit: it will give you a more objective view of yourself, and you will get some reading from your intimates on whether your obsessive behavior is torpedoing your friendships.

2. Examine your ethical and spiritual priorities. Are you working at such a frenzy because the job is actually that important to you, or has it become simply a way of living, a habitual compulsion, the reasons for which are obsolete? You may be able to find some activities which are generally considered humane and edifying— the great works and achievements in art, music, spirituality, philosophy, history, and science—which will help you retrieve your deeper self.

3. Spend some time outdoors. Nature has an important calming effect, and too many urban people go for days without taking note of the weather, the color of the trees, the movement of the stars. I believe we were all made to be outdoors for part of every day, and it is my goal to take a long look at the sky every few hours, including a stroll outdoors every evening to see what stars are in place. One need not live in the country to enjoy nature. Thoreau was once asked why, being a nature lover, he did not travel more widely. "There is more of nature between my front door and the front gate than I will ever be able to observe in a lifetime," he replied.

To a hypochondriac niece, the somber philosopher Søren Kierkegaard wrote: "Above all, do not lose your desire to walk. Every day I walk myself into my best thoughts, and I know of no thought so burdensome that one cannot walk away from it."

4. Become deliberate in the way you control your schedule. Decide on the time of day you should stop work and begin to enjoy some other pleasures. If you have worked until 7:00 each evening, you may have forgotten why you work that late every day. See if your schedule can be juggled so that you can come home at 5:30 three nights a week. Plan on some events, such as symphonies and visits to museums, that will enrich you and get you off the driven track.

5. Try out some new habits. In their book on Type A behavior, the authors suggest teaching yourself new habits. For instance, if you find yourself stepping on the accelerator to speed through a yellow light, take a penalty and turn right at the next corner, going back and going through the light in a more leisurely way. Such tricks will soon change your overall pace.

6. Take time for the people who are important. I, who am always in a hurry, had to suck in my breath for a moment upon reading these sentences from Paul Tournier: "When we open the Gospel we see that Jesus Christ, whose responsibilities were far greater than ours, seemed to be in much less of a hurry." He had plenty of time to speak to a foreign woman he met at a well, time to spend holidays with his disciples, time to admire the lilies of the field or a sunset, time to wash his disciples' feet, and time to answer their naive questions without impatience.

7. Strive to become flexible. If you find yourself on the freeway in the evening, stuck in traffic, fuming at the delay, remind yourself of several facts: your automaker has gone to great lengths to provide a seat that is probably more plush and more comfortable than the one to which you are headed at home, your car is probably climate controlled and filled with stereo music, so relax and enjoy this opportunity for renewal, contemplation, and recharging your emotional batteries.

8. Carve out time for play. By "play" I do not mean what men mean when they say, "I work hard and I play hard" (a typical remark of the competitive, driven person). Rather, I mean time to splash in the waves at the beach with a five-year-old, time to throw your dog the Frisbee, time to become like little children, as Jesus urged.

9. Devote yourself to regular spiritual disciplines. The people I admire always turn out to be people who practice rigorously the habit of a daily appointment with God. I once asked Dr. Louis Evans Sr., at that time pastor of the largest Presbyterian church in the world, "What is your secret?" Without blinking he said, "McGinnis, you can't give out without taking in." And he went on to explain that he arrived at his study by 7:00 each morning and took no calls until 11:00. Those hours were devoted to prayer and study. People who, in Emerson's noble phrase, "live from a great depth of being," have always required time to contemplate, time to listen for guidance, to bask awhile in the awareness that we are cloaked in the love of God.

What is needed for the driven, obsessive worker, is to shift the basic criterion for self-value away from *doing* and *having* and toward *being*. We are of value not for what we accomplish but rather because we are children of God. No more and no less a reason is necessary for us to feel confident. When that foundation is established for our worth, we begin to discover a balance between work and play and love.

An anonymous friar in a Nebraska monastery wrote the following late in life:

If I had my life to live over again,
I'd try to make more mistakes next time.
I would relax, I would limber up,
I would be sillier than I have been this trip.
I would take more trips. I would be crazier.
I would climb more mountains, swim more rivers,
    and watch more sunsets.
I would do more walking and looking.
I would eat more ice cream and less beans.

FOUR FUNDAMENTALS FOR SELF-CONFIDENCE
■

If I had to do it over again I would go places,
do things, and travel lighter.
If I had my life to live over I would start barefooted
earlier in the spring and stay that way later in the
fall.
I would ride on more merry-go-rounds.
I'd pick more daisies.

CONFIDENCE
■ ■ ■ ■ ■ ■ ■ ■ ■
CHAPTER FOUR

One does not "find oneself" by pursuing one's self,
but on the contrary by pursuing something else
and learning through discipline or routine . . .
who one is and wants to be.

—MAY SARTON

Aiming for
Personal Excellence

I SAID IN THE LAST CHAPTER that if your identity
is too closely tied to production, you are in trouble.
But now we must look at the other side of that coin,
for one's accomplishments have considerable importance for developing a strong sense of personal worth.
At lunch one day with writer Arthur Gordon I was
expounding on the importance of self-image. I tried
out on him the thesis of the last chapter—that we are
of value not so much for doing as for being.

He smiled and said, "We aren't created merely 'to
be.' We were made to be *something,* to accomplish
something. I don't mean you have to be the world's
foremost pianist—you can be generous or be kind—

but people are not going to come to the end of life and feel worth anything unless they have done something with their lives.''

He was right, of course. We will have a strong self-image only when we identify our talents and use them diligently. This may sound contradictory to what I've been saying about workaholics who try to establish their worth by working hard. The distinction we must keep in mind is this: our value does not come from our accomplishments, our accomplishments are the result of our intrinsic worth. That is, if we have some confidence in ourselves because we are created by a loving God—because we are God's children, made in our Father's image—then we will want to accomplish something with our gifts. We will want to do something that will last.

The bonus we receive is that as we accomplish something worthwhile, our self-esteem is enhanced. We are more than what we do, but what we do constitutes a significant part of who we are. No one has ever had healthy self-respect who did not have a sense of purpose in life, and Karl Menninger (among others) said that to be well-adjusted one must have some play, some love, and some work.

So here is the fourth fundamental for developing self-confidence:

FIND SOMETHING YOU LIKE TO DO AND DO WELL, THEN DO IT OVER AND OVER

In *Getting Rich Your Own Way*, Dr. Srully Blotnick relates a study of 1500 men and women who were followed for 20 years, from their early twenties to their early forties. Of those 1500, 83 became millionaires in that time. Three or four characteristics stood out in these persons. They had not set out to become wealthy. Most of the others had at one time or another tried to make a lot of money, and between them they had tried every get-rich-quick scheme in the world. They had tried investments and pyramid plans, and none of them had made it.

In this study, every one of those who became wealthy decided very early to specialize and do something that absorbed them totally—something that they loved to do. And in specializing and doing what they loved to do over the years, they became very, very good at it. As a result, they were paid well. (They also had another characteristic—they didn't throw their money around, as many of the others in the study did. They invested carefully.) Then lo and behold, they lifted up their heads after 15 or 20 years of hard work and discovered that their net worth was over a million dollars. They were so busy doing what they loved to do, so busy being excellent at what they were doing, that they were hardly aware of how wealthy they were becoming. Seventy to eighty percent of these people were working for a salary for a company. They weren't entrepreneurs and weren't great technical geniuses. But they worked for a company that could pay them well for doing one thing in an extraordinary fashion.

There are two essential steps to putting this principle into practice:

1. Assess your talents to determine where it is you can make a telling contribution.

2. Undertake the hard task of practice and improvement so that you become excellent at one thing.

Assessing Your Gifts

As a psychotherapist who sees many disturbed and disadvantaged people, I can still say that in every person, no matter how handicapped, there is some particular talent.

Horace Bushnell, the great New England preacher, used to say, "Somewhere under the stars God has a job for you to do and nobody else can do it." Some of us must find our place by trial and error, and it can take time, with a lot of dead ends along the way, but the talent is there, however buried. We are an important part of God's plan.

I have long admired Washington D.C.'s Church of the Savior, in part because they place such an emphasis on calling forth one another's gifts. Almost as soon as you begin worshiping there, you are confronted with the question, "What are your gifts?" The congregation sees this as another way of saying, "What is your call?"

Thomas Merton said, "Each one of us has some kind of vocation. We are all called by God to share in His life and in His kingdom. Each one of us is called to a special place in the kingdom. If we find that place we will be happy. If we do not find it, we can never be completely happy."

In discovering this call, it seems to me that we can

go awry at two points. First, we can wait for some dramatic revelation of God's plan for our lives, instead of seeing that God's blueprint for us is often written on our natures—it is obvious from the gifts that are within us. Second, we can get discouraged because our talents seem limited and others seem more skilled than we are. Usually it is not raw talent but *drive* that makes people successful.

The Law of Compensation

Those with a high level of confidence may have as many or more weaknesses than those with lower self-esteem. The difference is this: instead of dwelling on their handicaps, they compensate for them by building on their strengths.

In a famous study by Victor and Mildred Goertzel, entitled *Cradles of Eminence,* the home backgrounds of 300 highly successful people were investigated. These 300 subjects had made it to the top. They were men and women whose names everyone would recognize as brilliant in their fields, such as Franklin D. Roosevelt, Helen Keller, Winston Churchill, Albert Schweitzer, Clara Barton, Gandhi, Einstein, and Freud. The intensive investigation into their early home lives yielded some surprising findings:

■ Three-fourths of the children were troubled either by poverty, by a broken home, or by rejecting, overpossessive, or dominating parents.

■ Seventy-four of 85 writers of fiction or drama and 16 of the 20 poets came from homes where, as children, they saw tense psychological drama played out by their parents.

▪ Physical handicaps such as blindness, deafness, or crippled limbs characterized over one-fourth of the sample.

How did these people go on, then, to such outstanding accomplishments? Most likely by compensation. They compensated for their weaknesses in one area by excelling in another. One person talked about the forces that made him successful: "What has influenced my life more than any other single thing has been my stammer. Had I not stammered I would probably have gone to Cambridge as my brothers did, perhaps have become a don and every now and then published a dreary book about French Literature." The speaker (who stammered until his death) was W. Somerset Maugham, as he looked back on his life at age 86. By then he had become a world-renowned author of more than 20 books, 30 plays, and scores of essays and short stories.

Helping Kids Excel

The strategy of compensation is also something parents can employ. Dr. James Dobson tells about his young junior high years, when he was skinny and shy and not very popular. But when he was not quite eight, his father had taken him out to a tennis court one Saturday with a bucket of balls and began to teach him to play tennis. The Saturday workout became a ritual, and "at times," says Dobson, "I got bored with it and did not want to practice. But my dad kept his thumb in my back and we were out there every Saturday morning. Well, I am glad he did because when I was in junior high school and feeling very shy and inferior, if asked to write an essay on the subject, 'Who I Am,' the one positive thing I could have said was 'I am the best tennis player in my school.' "

Late Bloomers

It takes some people a long while to discover and deploy their gifts, and if you find yourself unaccomplished at middle-age or after, it does not mean that you are ungifted. Helen Yglesias, for instance, was 54 years old when she finished her first book.

When Yglesias was a teenager, in the early depression, she had hopes of being a great writer and had even started a book based on her teenage experiences. But after her older brother read the manuscript, his reactions hit her like shrapnel. "I don't remember much of what we said to one another, or if I answered him at all. I remember the word 'perverted.' 'Nobody in the world is going to be interested in that perverted stuff you're writing.' And 'you'd have to be a genius to get away with this boring stuff, and you're no genius.' " In tears she shredded her manuscript page by page.

Although the incident took its toll, Helen Yglesias says that many other forces also contributed to four decades of literary inactivity. One day she was discussing the 40-year delay in her writing with author Christina Stead, who told her to stop talking about it and start writing. "Just sit down and write the book you mean to write," she instructed. "That's the way it's done. You'll either succeed in handling the material, or you'll fail. If you fail, do it again until you get it right. Of course, there's more to it than that . . . but the details are nonsense until you sit down to work."

Yglesias says that when she began working on her book she felt "a sense of having taken my true life into my hands at long last." When the book became a success, she went on to publish novels such as *Family Feeling* and *Sweetsir,* and memoirs such as *Starting Early, Anew, Over and Late,* which have made her a highly-respected author.

"The world stands aside," said David Jordan, "to let anyone pass who knows where he is going." This applies to those who learn where they are going late in life as well as for the young. At age 53, Margaret Thatcher became Britain's first female prime minister. At 64, Francis Chichester sailed alone around the world in a 53-foot yacht. At 65, Winston Churchill became British prime minister for the first time and started the epic struggle against Hitler. At 71, Golda Meir became prime minister of Israel. At 75, Ed Delano of California bicycled 3100 miles in 33 days to attend his 50th college reunion in Worcester, Massachusetts. At 76, Cardinal Angelo Roncalli became Pope John XXIII and inaugurated major changes in his church. At 80, Grandma Moses, who had started painting in her late 70s, had her first one-woman exhibit. At 81, Benjamin Franklin skillfully mediated between disagreeing factions at the U.S. Constitutional Convention. At 80, Winston Churchill returned to the House of Commons as a member of parliament and also exhibited 62 of his paintings. At 96, George C.

Selbach scored a 110-yard hole-in-one at Indian River, Michigan. And on his 100th birthday, ragtime pianist Eubie Blake exclaimed, "If I'd known I was going to live this long, I'd have taken better care of myself."

Dogged Devotion to Your Gift

There is nothing more common than unsuccessful people who have talent, and for many of us, the problem has not been a difficulty in discovering an area of natural aptitude. Rather, it has been in the development of that skill. It is the boring, repetitive sharpening of our skills that will place us beyond the masses.

Many of us get interested in a field, but then the going gets tough, we see that other people are more successful, and we get discouraged and quit. I once counseled a woman who had been largely unfocused throughout much of her lifetime. I asked how she would describe her life. "Regret," she said, simply. Then she went on to talk about the years when she meandered from one thing to another, never taking an inventory of her abilities and deciding on a speciality.

"My husband didn't care whether I worked, so I didn't, and that was probably my biggest mistake. When the kids got older and didn't need me as much, I kept thinking I'd find something. I got bored with piano lessons and quit. I thought I might become a teacher and took some courses in education, but didn't stay long enough to get a credential. I can't tell you how terrible it is to come to the last third of your life and feel that you're not good at anything but baking good apple pies.'' All of us have known able persons who flitted from one thing to another, getting bored with this, disenchanted with that, and never buckling down to excel.

The work of a surgeon is based on the most minute breakdown of the job into individual motions. Young surgeons practice for months on end to tie a certain knot in a confined space, to change and hold an instrument, or to make stitches. There is a constant effort to improve these motions, to speed up by a fraction of a second, to make another one easier, to eliminate a third one. And the improvement of these individual, constituent motions is the surgeon's main method of improving total performance. That is scientific management, and it serves as a splendid model for the management of our gifts.

A few years ago I met a master furniture maker who has become very good at a very specialized thing: making custom furniture. When Sam Maloof was a young man he had training in design, but learned that what he liked best was to work with his hands in wood. So he began making furniture in his garage.

At first, as he experimented with the joints that would later make him famous, he made a prototype chair, then took it up to the roof of his garage and dropped it to the driveway to see if the joints would take the stress, which they did. This proved to Sam that he was using the proper type of joinery. His first commission was for a dining room set, and because of problems with the interior decorator, the total price barely covered his materials. But by trial and error he learned how to price his work so he could make a living.

Word of Maloof's craftsmanship spread, and he began to get more jobs. Because of zoning problems, he bought a lemon grove away from the city with a small house and garage in the middle of the grove. There he continued to make chairs from walnut, all superbly handcrafted. At first, commissions came in slowly, and during this same period he was asked by the U.S. State Department to go to Lebanon, Iran, and later to El Salvador to work with woodworkers of those countries in village industry programs.

But over the years the furniture maker's fame spread. He added an apprentice. He built a workshop and a house, room by room. As his chairs became famous, various furniture manufacturers offered to buy his designs and cheaply produce thousands of the rockers per month. But Maloof was not interested in licensing his designs. He continued to improve and perfect his work. He knew what he liked to do, and that was building the best furniture that he could build.

As word of his craft spread, he was asked to hold workshops in furniture making, and many of his pieces were acquired by museums for their permanent collections. Recently he was the recipient of the MacArthur "genius" award, an honor usually granted to writers, artists, and philosophers. It will give Maloof a tax-free, no-strings-attached stipend of $60,000 a year for five years.

And what has the "genius award" done to Sam Maloof's working week? Scarcely changed it at all. He is 71 now, and still works about 60 hours a week.

FOUR FUNDAMENTALS FOR SELF-CONFIDENCE

He has two assistants. The present price of his rocker? $6000, and he has back orders for well over a hundred. "That's why I have to work so many hours," he says, smiling.

Maloof's sense of satisfaction and well-being stems in part from his work: he knows exactly who he is, and he does the things that are a natural expression of himself. He found something to do, did it over and over, and became better and better at it.

PART
. . . . . .
TWO

DAILY EXERCISES FOR BUILDING SELF-CONFIDENCE

CONFIDENCE
· · · · · · · · ·
CHAPTER FIVE

*The only difference between
the best performance and the worst performance
is the variation in our self-talk.*

—DOROTHY AND BETTE HARRIS

Improving
Your Inner Dialog

JAMES JOYCE'S CLASSIC NOVEL *Ulysses* depicts the stream of consciousness moving through the mind of Leopold Bloom and others during a 24-hour period. Joyce's work makes poignantly clear that even when we are not talking to others, we are always carrying on a conversation with ourselves.

If I could plug a set of headphones into the minds of my clients and listen in on the statements they make to themselves all day, I am convinced that the majority of them would be negative: "I'm running late again—as usual." "My hair looks terrible this morning." "That was a stupid remark to have made—she probably thinks I'm a dummy." By the thousands these messages flash across our brains every day, and it is small wonder that the results are diminished self-image.

One good daily exercise for building self-confidence, then, is to practice a more friendly inner dialog:

REPLACE SELF-CRITICISM WITH REGULAR, POSITIVE SELF-TALK

Donald Meichenbaum has developed a sophisticated way to help persons change their stream of inner conversation. Here, for instance, is the way an impulsive and highly self-critical child might approach an assignment:

Oh boy, this is going to be tough. I'm going to make a mess of this for sure. Oh! there you go, you've already made a mistake. I never could draw. Stupid, you were supposed to go *down* there. He'll see where I've erased that. It looks as if others are doing fine on theirs, but this is a mess. That's as good as I can do, but it's not what they want.

Here is the way Meichenbaum trains the same child to talk within:

Okay, what is it I have to do? You want me to copy the picture with the different lines. I have to go slow and be careful. Okay, draw the line down, down, *good;* then to the right, *that's it;* now down some more and to the left. *Good, I'm doing fine so far.* Remember go slow. Now back up again. *No, I was supposed to go down. That's okay.* Just erase the line carefully . . . carefully. Okay, I have to go down now. *Finished. I did it.*

Such a method of talking to ourselves can be a great help in reprogramming our self-image.

The Origins of Self-Criticism

Where did we learn to talk to ourselves with recrimination? We learned it from other people, of course. The thousands of negative messages that came from parents and teachers and older siblings, as they tried to turn us into socially acceptable beings, are all stored in our memories. Many of those messages get assimilated into the general patter of conversation we carry on with ourselves all day. "Why are you always late? . . . What's the matter with you, do you want to get run over? . . . This way, idiot. . . . Can't you even catch the ball?"

A few years ago I was returning from a speaking engagement late in the evening, and the flight from Dallas to Los Angeles was the longest of my life. A mother and her little three-year-old daughter were sitting behind me, and the girl was restless. The mother was irritable, and again and again she said:

"Can't you sit still for a while?

"You do *not* have to go to the bathroom. I'm tired of your bothering me.

"You make me sick.

"If you don't stop being so bad, I'm going to have your father spank you when we get home."

The closer we got to Los Angeles, the more desperate the mother got, until her messages were:

"You're being a pest. Just be quiet.

"You're the worst behaved kid on this airplane. Shut up.

"You're a bad girl, and I'm going to take you to the restroom and give you the spanking of your life if you're not quiet."

I wanted to turn around and say to the little girl, "Honey, you're not bad. It's just that your mother's tired and you're tired." For that stream of derogatory messages was being internalized and will become a part of the girl's conversation with herself.

We learn from the evaluations of the people around us, and some psychologists go so far as to say that we know ourselves only from the mirror of other people's reactions to us. If someone says, "You have trouble with math, don't you?" it is normal to assume—if such persons are bigger and older and wiser—that they're right. Then for the rest of our lives, whenever a set of numbers appears before our eyes, our automatic response is, "Remember, you always have trouble with math."

Talking More Positively
to Children

These facts make it all the more important that we pump as much positive material as possible into the young minds around us. Of course, we must correct our children and our students when they make mistakes, but we can do it with positive messages:

"You're a smart guy—you can see that it's dangerous to swing the bat here in the house."

"This is not like you. Your work is usually so neat. I want you to do that page over."

"You're one of the best-behaved girls in the class, Joan. What's wrong today that you're talking so much?"

"I love you, Tom, but you're making me nervous tonight."

Such an approach to parenting and teaching will reap good dividends in the future, because the result will be a much more positive stream of consciousness in those children. They will grow up to say such things as:

"I'm no dummy. I can figure this one out with a little time."

"This is not like me. Got to figure out what's wrong so I can get back to normal production."

"I like getting along with people, and always feel good when I walk into this office. I'm pretty well accepted around here, and that feels good."

The Principle of Displacement

But let's say that you have not been so fortunate in your past and that you have absorbed a thousand depreciating messages and you are in the habit of saying to yourself, "I'm no good at math," or "I'm a hothead, and my anger is going to get me in trouble one of these days." Can anything be done about this habit? Certainly. We can start by following the law of displacement. The way to get rid of negative messages is to so fill our minds with good thoughts that the negative ones are necessarily displaced.

Like everything else, we will learn to talk to ourselves more kindly with practice. As we're driving to work, for instance, we can experiment with a positive stream of material such as,

OK, I'm going to learn to talk to myself better today. What can I say that's good? Well, I'm on time this morning, that feels good. Nice not to have to hurry, can be a little more courteous to the other commuters today. When I stop and think about it, I like to be considerate, wait for the other driver to pull in if she's in a hurry. Always have gotten a lot of pleasure from doing little favors like that. It's the big favors I resent doing. Whoops. There was a typical put-down I make so often. How can I frame that more positively? I can say this: I'd like to get in the habit of doing more big favors for people. Could probably get as much pleasure from them as I just did in letting the woman pass.

Work today—how does that look? What positive messages can I give myself here to get in a good frame of mind? Well, for starters, I wrote more orders last month than ever before. Joe is probably happy about that. Come to think of it, I'm a pretty important cog in that operation. I think I help the morale there. Got to keep remembering what Patti said last week about my cheering the place up. That was a nice compliment. Not overstated if I do say so myself. But let's get back to work this morning. I really don't mind going to the office most days. In fact I can put it stronger than that: I like the place. Hate the paper work. Whoops, there's another of those zingers. Let's turn that around: I bet I can get the paperwork pile finished up before lunch today. That would make lunch more enjoyable. Seeing Tom for lunch. I always look forward to that. He seems to listen to my opinions. If he can swing it, I believe he'd like to give me their entire account.

The Habit of Self-Depreciation

Many people apologize constantly and make lots of self-depreciating remarks to others because they get secondary gain from it. Let me illustrate. A man has a normal day at work, feeling some fatigue, but in general he is quite energized during his last conversation on the telephone. He closes his office and drives home. As he emerges from the garage and walks toward the front door, it's as if a debilitating fatigue comes over him, and his shoulders visibly sag. He can't wait to pour a drink and collapse on the couch.

What has come over this man? In this case, his wife has set him up to come home exhausted every night because she is so sympathetic about his tough job. She assumes her most attentive, loving manner when she thinks he's had a hard day, and the consequence is that he comes home tired a great deal. It's not that he's being dishonest and leading her on. He is not saying within himself, "I feel fine, but I'll see if I can get some extra attention by playing tired." He genuinely feels terrible fatigue on the way from the garage to the front door. But it is for the secondary gain.

Our bodies will play strange tricks on us and we will put up with enormous actual pain in order to get some sympathy and love—if that's the only way we know to get it. So this man talks about how tired he is as he comes in the door, reiterates what a stressful day it has been, and uses words like *exhausted*, *frazzled*, *stressed*, and *tired* a few times, and sure enough, he can barely move. These negative thoughts keep coming through his consciousness, he makes himself more and more tired, and before 9:00 he's passed out on the couch.

How can all that debilitating talk be reversed? The man could say something like this:

Nice to be coming home after a long day. Feel OK, though. Refuse to give in to fatigue tonight. I'm not going to say a word to Marge about being tired. Neck's a little stiff, but the kinks are leaving as I roll my head a little. Lawn looks great. Must remember to tell her how nice the new flowers look. Her car's in the garage. Gosh it's great to have a wife who's always home waiting for me. Bet we could make some love tonight. Sex is still exciting with her after all these years. The old body still functions fine, and that's a lot to be thankful for. Going to pass on a drink tonight. Just makes me tired, and I don't need anything to relax. Good decision. Nice going. Trying to remember to give myself a conscious pat on the back for stuff like that. I'm going to walk in that door with a little bounce to my step. She deserves to have someone who cheers her up instead of bringing in a bagful of fatigue. Gosh I love that woman. Remarkable, really, that a few strong, encouraging remarks like this could make me feel so much better. Pretty powerful machine, this brain of ours.

Does such a process sound falsely positive? If so, you will want to adapt your own inner dialog so that it fits you. But whatever you do, make a conscious decision that you will send a stream of enthusiastic, vital, encouraging messages through your mind. It may amaze you to discover what power exists in that three-pound powerhouse on your shoulders.

Statements of Hope

One way to get in the habit of running a more optimistic stream of self-dialog through your brain is to put it on paper. As in prayer, our minds easily wander, and just as some of us find it easier to pray by writing out our prayers—as if we were writing a letter to God—so writing positive statements helps focus our attention.

The process is in many ways very similar to prayer. Here's how it works. In your journal each day, preferably early in the morning, you can write a few statements such as these:

- I feel optimistic about the day that is unfolding.
- I am a competent decision maker and trust that I'll do the right things as I go through this day.
- I enjoy nature and feel good as I look out this window at the misty morning.
- My body is God's creation, and I'm going to enjoy the sensations it sends me today.

These are not so much goals for the day as statements of belief, which repeated again and again can change how we feel about ourselves.

I know of no better material for these exercises than the great statements of hope from the Scriptures. If it is true that we become what we think about, then it will change the core of our being to memorize and repeat again and again such affirmations as these:

"The Lord is my light and my salvation—whom shall I fear?" (Ps. 27:1).

"Those who hope in the Lord will renew their strength" (Isa. 40:31).

"In all things God works for the good of those who love him" (Rom. 8:28).

"I can do everything through him who gives me strength" (Phil. 4:13).

CONFIDENCE

· · · · · · · · ·

CHAPTER SIX

*The mightiest works have been
accomplished by men who have somehow kept
their ability to dream great dreams.*

—WALTER RUSSELL BOWIE

Imagination is more important than knowledge.

—ALBERT EINSTEIN

Envisioning a Confident Self

THERE IS A SECOND DAILY EXERCISE for building self-esteem that recently has been employed with considerable success by athletes. It is variously called "mental rehearsal," "imaging," "visualization," and "visioning," and it is anything but a new discovery. The idea is as old as the Bible. Here it is:

· ·

REPLACE FEAR OF FAILURE WITH CLEAR PICTURES OF YOURSELF FUNCTIONING SUCCESSFULLY AND HAPPILY

· ·

In October 1979, Dr. Charles Garfield, an associate clinical professor at the University of California School

82

of Medicine, attended a medical symposium in Milan, Italy. There he got into a conversation with some European scientists who had spent 20 years and millions of dollars doing research on how to train athletes for optimum performance. After they talked into the night about the scientists' discoveries on the power of guided imagery, Dr. Garfield became very interested and offered himself as a research subject. The group woke the local gym owner at 2:00 A.M. They had convinced Garfield that they could substantially increase his weight lifting ability merely by using certain psychological techniques. First he bench-pressed, with great difficulty, 300 pounds, while hooked up to their sophisticated monitors which were measuring brain waves, the heart, and muscle tension.

They asked how much he thought he might lift if he were in a meet and strained to his highest capacity. He replied, "Maybe 310 pounds."

"They then put me through some very deep relaxation exercises," says Garfield, "and asked me to imagine in my mind successfully lifting not 300 pounds but a 20% increase. After 40 minutes of what seemed to be very repetitive mental rehearsal, they asked me to try the barbell on which they had placed what looked like a lot of extra weight. After one false start, I made the lift considerably easier than I had made the 300. It was not until then that they told me I had just bench-pressed 365 pounds! According to their calibrations they thought they could easily take me up to 400, but did not do so out of deference to my out-of-shape muscles."

The process used by these sports psychologists is based on the fact that we do not think in words but in pictures. So athletes play movies over and over in their minds—movies in which they see themselves hitting the perfect drive or soaring over the bar.

This technique is equally valuable for the person with low self-confidence. In order to succeed you must see yourself succeeding. In order to become more confident, you must picture yourself as a person with high self-esteem. You play movies of yourself approaching a difficult challenge and you see yourself coming to it with poise and confidence. When we burn such pictures into our minds powerfully enough, they become a part of the unconscious, and we begin to expect to succeed.

Some Christian writers recently have attacked this mental imaging as being somehow occult and non-Christian, but nothing could be further from the truth. The Scriptures admonish us again and again to pray with faith, and explain that the answer to our prayers will be in proportion to our belief. This way of "seeing" the event occur is one very concrete way of exercising that faith.

We who have long downgraded ourselves also play movies in our minds, but the movies are ones of failure. We play over and over the scenes of past disasters, and when we are facing some challenge, we worry in the same way. Remember, the mind thinks in pictures and symbols, not words. So as we worry, we are seeing scenes of ourselves failing. We can sometimes be quite vivid in imagining this failure. We see ourselves embarrassed, flopping, standing with egg on our faces. The rerunning of these tapes in our heads becomes a habit, and it then affects all our behavior. Norman Cousins once wrote, "People are never more insecure than when they become obsessed with their fears at the expense of their dreams.''

Let's say you are headed for the office and you know it's going to be a busy, demanding day. As you drive to work, it is easy to begin picturing what it will be like: people with jangled nerves, a lot of problems coming at you thick and fast. You will be stressed and fatigued, the afternoon will drag, and you won't be able to wait until quitting time. The movie is playing in your mind as vividly as if you were sitting before a television screen.

Someone has said that we may not get what we want, but we will get what we *expect*. And if we expect to have a terrible day, filled with tension and problems, we'll very likely have just the kind of day we pictured. If, on the other hand, we can vividly see ourselves enjoying the challenges of the day, working without strain and tension, enjoying the people with whom we are associated, laughing at certain incongruities when they come, and successfully dealing with a multitude of difficulties, it is much more likely that our day will resemble that picture. Louis E. Tice, head of Pacific Institute, calls this the law of focused attention: What you hold in your mind is what you move toward.

Tice goes on to say that the important questions are ones such as these:

- How do I want my future to look?
- How would I picture my marriage functioning at its best?
- What will our new house look like?
- Just how would I picture an ideal evening with my family?

▪ How do I see my business operating ideally?

Since we are like living magnets, if we can picture these scenes strongly enough and often enough, they have an uncanny way of coming true. A famous restauranteur was asked, "When did you start to succeed?"

"I was succeeding when I was sleeping on park benches," he replied, "because I knew what I wanted to do, and could picture my successful restaurant and exactly how it was the best dining establishment in town. It was simply a matter of time before the picture came true."

Thomas Watson Sr. was 40 years old when he became general manager of a little firm that made meat slicers, time clocks, and primitive tabulators. He recognized the potential of a machine for processing and storing information—a computer—a decade before its first commercial use. To match his mission, he soon renamed his little company International Business Machines Corporation. When asked toward the end of his life at what point he envisioned IBM as being so huge and successful, he answered, "Right at the beginning."

A man named George Lopez told me of his years of growing up in a barrio of Los Angeles. He said that he lived to fight in those days.

I would drive down to San Pedro, the port area, park my Ford, and lean against it waiting for some gang member to pick a fight, just so I could sharpen my skills. In high school I never studied, so I made mostly Ds, then when I was a senior a couple of my friends said they were going to college.

"College, what's that?" I asked.

"Well, college, that's where you go after high school," they shrugged.

So I decided I'd go to be with my friends, and the next fall found myself in the local community college. I had no study habits and cut classes just as I always had, so within a few weeks I was on my way to getting dropped, which was okay with me until a history professor, Donald R. Haydu, took an interest for some reason and began to talk to me about my possibilities. No teacher had ever talked to me like that before. Through some complicated maneuvers, I decided the next semester that I was going to be a doctor. I'll never forget the day I decided that. I had figured out that it would cost $55,000 for the education and I had 44 cents in my pocket. My father was opposed to my going to school and had already told me he couldn't help, but I knew that somehow, someway, I was going to become a doctor.

When I took organic chemistry, I was far behind all the other students, so I would read the chapter ahead of time, then go through and try to work the problems. Then I'd try to work them backwards. I still didn't understand much of it, but kept going over and over the material, so that when I walked into the lecture, I'd gone through it three or four times. Then, hearing the lecture, I'd ask good questions and it would fall into place.

I'd go to school at 8 A.M. and would not leave the campus until the library closed at 11 P.M. Walking home at night, I'd picture myself as a doctor. "George Lopez, M.D." I'd see myself examining patients and operating. I'd picture my name on the door: "George Lopez, M.D.," and I'd see myself bringing about new medical advances. Over and over I'd play those tapes, and that, I'm convinced was what enabled me to wake up early the next morning energized.

The result? George Lopez, M.D., finished his medical education with distinction, soon became head of a large group of practicing physicians, and now owns the company that markets six medical patents which he has developed, and which will save hundreds of lives in the next decade.

Here are some practical suggestions for positive visualization:

1. Find a Regular Time and Place

Those who practice mental rehearsal usually put aside 15 to 20 minutes a day for positive imaging, as did Lopez. This can be done while commuting to work, at lunch, early in the morning, or at the end of the day, as it was for him. But it is important to have a regular time and setting to help you fall into the reveries of this exercise. Picture yourself in one sequence making a business conquest, and savor the experience. Perhaps in another picture you will want to see yourself happily ensconced with your family, and in another you might picture yourself relishing some athletic victory or weighing in at your desired weight. We must be relentless in playing these movies over and over, for negative states of thought can get firmly embedded and it takes regular practice over a long period to transform those into confident ways of approaching the future.

2. Picture the Event Occurring in the Present

Do not engage in vague daydreaming about some future never-never land. Instead, picture the scene as if it were occurring right now. By the time Thomas Fatjo was 36 years old, he had turned $500 and a used garbage truck into the country's biggest solid-waste-disposal company. Fatjo gives the credit for much of this success to what he calls "creative dreaming." "For instance," he writes, "in the beginning stages of developing our first garbage company in Houston, I used to imagine trucks, a whole fleet of blue trucks, running out of our lot onto the streets of Houston in the early morning mist. In my imagination I could 'see' the trucks and the men as they wound their way around the streets of our town.

"These times of dreaming were not spent engaged in the planning process, figuring out how to implement these fantasies. *Rather, in my imagination I held dream-pictures of the goals being already accomplished.*"

3. Enlist the Senses

Those who are able to visualize the future most positively use their five senses to get as much detail as possible. Hear the sounds of the event, feel the sensations of experiencing the triumph, try to smell success in the air as it is happening. For example, let's say you have a problem relaxing in social settings.

Envision yourself at a party where you hear the children happily playing in another room. Take in the sight and smell of the carefully prepared floral arrangement. Taste the food at dinner, and see yourself functioning with confidence and pleasure.

4. Be Realistic in Your Vision

If you cannot visualize your dream occurring with vivid detail, then you need to scale it down. Louis Tice now owns a multimillion-dollar company that does seminars on excellence for many Fortune 500 companies. "When I was earning $20,000 a year as a school teacher," says Tice, "it would have been pie-in-the-sky for me to visualize the annual income I now make. If you can't imagine vividly what it would be like to be making $500,000 a year, then what can you picture? $100,000? $30,000? When I was making less than $2,000 a month, I wondered what it would be like to make $2,500 and wondered if I could increase my income that much. Eventually I decided that yes I could, and began to picture it. Before long, of course, it happened. Then I began to imagine myself making $3,000, and on and on."

Some leaders are guilty of overpromising, saying that if you believe enough and work hard enough you can have anything. These are ridiculous platitudes. But in reacting against such careless talk, we can easily throw the baby out with the bathwater and stop dreaming, which is fatal.

In an interview soon after Neil Armstrong's historic first step on the moon, he said, "Ever since I was a

little boy, I dreamed I would do something important
in aviation."

PART
......
THREE

STEPS
TO
INDEPENDENCE

Do not conform any longer
to the pattern of this world,
but be transformed by the renewing of your mind.

—ROMANS 12:2

I cannot give you the formula for success
but I can give you the formula for failure,
which is: Try to please everybody.

—HERBERT BAYARD SWOPE

Breaking Away from Other People's Expectations

SYDNEY J. HARRIS was walking in New York City one evening with a friend, a Quaker, who stopped to buy a newspaper. The newsboy was surly and discourteous as he made change, but Harris's friend looked him in the eye and gave him a warm greeting as he left.

"A sullen fellow, isn't he?" Harris asked.

"Oh, he's that way every night," shrugged the friend.

"Then why do you continue to be so kind to him?" Harris asked.

"Why not?" his friend responded. "Why should I let him decide how I'm going to act?"

The Quaker obviously knew how to live independently. He was a person in possession of himself, with a solid center of gravity. It is such a center of gravity—an assurance of who we are and how we wish to live—that we must pursue if we are to develop genuine confidence.

Unfortunately, most of us are more reactive. We allow the people around us to determine our attitude by their behavior or expectations. This chapter and the one that follows are about the art of independence—how you can be your own person, living above the expectations and demands of people. The first step for independent living is this:

■■■

DARE TO BE A LITTLE ECCENTRIC
■■■

Those with strong self-confidence always have people they love and are close to, but they also have the courage to be different from those around them. We cannot live without the love of others. In fact, in a later chapter I will emphasize the importance of building a network of strong friendships to enhance your self-image. But that is quite different from a neurotic need to please others. There are many people who would like to impose on us certain conditions of worth, and to submit to them is to submit to a life of scrambling.

The Dangers of Trying to Please

Dr. Neil Clark Warren, former dean of the Fuller School of Psychology, says that we waste large amounts of psychological energy studying the important people in our lives, determining what they want from us, and then trying to become the kind of person who can meet all those needs.

If you buy into this strategy, calls come from every side. For instance, my mother wants me to be gentle and loving and nice. My dad wants me to be tough and confident and well-defined. My wife wants me to be a tiger: strong, successful, but sensitive. My friends want me to be open, and willing to be weak, but courageous. The students at our school want me to be well-prepared and well-reasoned and thoroughly competent and productive. The Seminary wants me to be conservative, but charitable; discriminating, and yet unconditional. They want me to be an effective fundraiser, an administrator and scholar and teacher. Society, I think, wants me to be masculine and sexually aware.

Sometimes I feel like crying out, "I just can't do it!" And somewhere I hear a voice, "If you can't do it, pretend." And the challenge to be a good pretender becomes the most challenging challenge of all. We create masks and learn parts. We make ourselves into actors and actresses and quick-change artists. We move from one part to another as rapidly as we meet some in our life who has differing expectations. Other people think we're amazing. They're so proud of us. They seek our company. They promote us and give us merit raises and hugs and trophies. We're so important to them but we have become strangers to ourselves. We have met everybody's needs but our own.

Returning to Your Center

The alternative to all this, according to Warren's felicitous phrase, is to "return to our center" and live from the authentic core within us. In psychoanalytic terms, it is seeing the *ego* as the decision-making entity, receiving the data from the *id*—our clamoring instinctual desires—and listening to the equally clamoring *super-ego,* which includes all the shoulds, oughts, and don'ts we have heard from countless important figures. The ego then makes its decisions from that strong center, which is our core. We are empowered to make those decisions, says Warren, by embracing the unconditional love that God has for us. When we embrace that experience of grace and live from such a center, we will refuse to let either our persistent instincts or the people around us control our lives with their expectations and demands.

It is a liberating step when we decide to stop being what other people want when it is pretense. Although the singer Risë Stevens had learned to work on the stage with great poise, the self-confidence she felt before audiences evaporated in social situations. She said, "My discomfort came from trying to be something I was not—a star in the drawing room as well as on stage. If a clever person made a joke, I tried to top it—and failed. I pretended to be familiar with subjects I knew nothing of."

After watching herself fail so desperately in this way, she had a heart-to-heart talk with herself: "I realized that I just simply wasn't a wit or an intellectual and that I could only succeed as myself. Then, facing my faults, I began listening and asking questions at parties instead of trying to impress the guests. I discovered that I had much to learn from others. When I spoke, I tried to contribute, not to shine. At once I began to feel a new warmth in my social contacts. . . . This brought me a new joy in being with people. They liked the real me better."

Are Women More Dependent on Relationships for Identity?

Most studies show that women have more difficulty establishing their singularity than men. The old stereotype is that men live for their work and women live for love; hence, when a relationship ends, a divorce occurs, or a friendship blows up, it is harder on women than on men.

Does that mean that women are by nature weaker and more dependent? Not at all. It has to do with the fact most small children spend more time during their early years with their mothers than they do with their fathers. Nancy Chodorow has done some illuminating work in this area. She points out that a little boy soon realizes that he is not like his mother and that he must differentiate himself from this person. Masculinity is defined by separation. A girl, on the other hand, feels no such need and remains close to her mother. These facts have great consequences for the way we cope when we become adults. Males often grow up being good at independence, but having trouble with closeness. Females often grow up being good at relationships but having problems with independence.

Between two and six times as many women as men are diagnosed as suffering from depression, and 70% of mood-altering drugs are taken by women. Why the difference? Maggie Scarf is probably right in suggesting a reason:

> Women are more depressed because they have been taught to be more dependent and affection-seeking, and thus they rarely achieve an independent sense of self. A woman gives her highest priorities to pleasing others, to being attractive to others, to being cared for, and to caring for others. Women receive ferocious training in a direction that leads away from thinking "What do I want?" and toward "What do *they* want?"

Such a dependent way of living leaves one very vulnerable. A woman's personality, still searching for a shape, may take the shape of those people around her. And so long as she is attractive to people and pleases the important figures in her life, her self-image is good. But let her marriage end or a friendship dissolve or her kids shut her out, and she may feel empty and alone.

Relationships are very important for healthy self-confidence, but we are in trouble if we base our value on how well we please the people around us. For sooner or later, most of us will find ourselves in some situation where it seems we are being criticized from all quarters.

Coping with Criticism

If we are to gain some sense of independence for ourselves, it is absolutely essential that we learn to handle criticism. Criticism is very difficult for some of us, and a person's self-image can be devastated by only one negative remark. But with practice, it is possible to learn how to stand secure in the face of our critics.

Winston Churchill once wrote about British General Tudor, who commanded a division facing the great German assault of March 1918: "The impression I had of Tudor was of an iron peg, hammered into the frozen ground, immovable." In the war the odds were heavily against him, but Tudor knew how to meet an apparently irresistible force. He merely stood firm and let the force expend itself on him. Such strength in the face of difficulties and criticism is necessary if we are to be confident and independent.

None of this is altogether new information. People are always telling us to live above criticism and to listen to our own drummer. But it is a long leap from good advice to actual independence. How, then, can you best assert your individuality? Here are some characteristics I have observed in people who lead healthy, nonconformist lives:

 • *They speak their minds*. Our conversations might be more interesting if we expressed our opinions more freely. Where, for instance, did we get the idea that in polite society you do not discuss politics and religion? How in the world are we going to have interesting talk *without* discussing politics and religion? There are cantankerous sorts who disagree merely to start an argument, and I'm not advocating that you be disagreeable out of principle. But for every person who does that, you can point to 200 souls who are boring because they try so hard not to offend anyone.

When Maggie Kuhn, former missionary and spokeswoman for the "Gray Panthers," was 76, I heard her speak about some of the infirmities of her age: "I have had cancer three times," she said, "and I'm fine. I also have arthritis in my fingers and knees, and I keep moving." To what did she attribute all this? To the liberty with which she expressed herself. "Old age is an excellent time for outrage," she said. "My goal is to say or do at least one outrageous thing every week."

▪ *They do a lot of experimenting.* Louis Fischer, the biographer of Gandhi, said that the great Indian leader always "reserved the right to differ with himself." His life was an unending experiment, and Fischer says that he was experimenting even in his seventies. "There was nothing stodgy about him. He was not a conforming Hindu or a conforming nationalist or a conforming pacifist. Gandhi was independent, unfettered, unpredictable, hence exciting and difficult. A conversation with him was a voyage of discovery: he dared to go anywhere without a chart."

▪ *They say no to others occasionally in order to say yes to themselves.* "I can't tell you how much of my life is spent at social engagements where I don't really want to be," a man said to me recently.

"Do you mean that these are social obligations required by your work?" I asked.

"No, they're things that friends or relatives are always inviting us to, and we don't want to hurt their feelings."

There are ways to say no with kindness. And even if at times we offend, that is better than living a saccharine life in which our actions are directed only by the desires of others. There are times when, in order to say yes to the best, we must say no to the good.

There also are times when, for the sake of our own identity, we must resist the efforts of people who want to manipulate us. Anthony Brandt tells of a woman who called a friend, asking him to contact her plumber and complain because the plumber hadn't installed the proper fixtures in her new bathroom. He thought it an odd request, but he could see that their friendship was at stake. He also could see that there was no sensible reason for him to act as a go-between for her; she ought to do her own complaining. He finally said no—and lost a friend. In such situations we can carefully explain that the request seems unreasonable, yet make clear that we care and do not want to lose the friendship. But when others make such compliance a condition of the relationship, then it may not be worth saving.

▪ *They are forever learning.* The great painter Renoir's last years were in some ways triumphant for him. Although he had been vilified as one of the early Impressionists, eventually he established a wide reputation, and art dealers from all over the world were competing for his work. And yet he would not stop painting. His son Jean wrote:

His body became more and more petrified. His hands with the fingers curled inwards could no longer pick up anything. . . . His skin had become so tender that contact with the wooden handle of the brush injured it. To avoid this difficulty he had a little piece of cloth inserted in the hollow of his hand. His twisted fingers gripped rather than held the brush. . . . It was under these conditions that he painted his "Women Bathers," now in the Louvre. He considered it the culmination of his life's work. He felt that in this picture he had summed up all his researches and prepared a spring-board from which he could plunge into further re-searches. . . . From his palette, simplified to the last degree, and from the minute "droppings" of color lost on its surface, issued a splendor of dazzling golds and purples, the glow of flesh filled with young and healthy blood, the magic of all-conquering light.

Jean Renoir also tells what his father was doing the day he died:

An infection which had developed in his lungs kept him to his room. He asked for his paintbox and brushes, and he painted the anemones which Nénette, our kind-hearted maid, had . . . gathered for him. For several hours he identified himself with these flowers, and forgot his pain. Then he motioned for someone to take his brush and said, "I think I am beginning to under-stand something about it."

"I think I am beginning to understand something about it"—a typical remark for a creative individualist. Re-gardless of their age, such people live on the edge of new knowledge, new fields, and new discoveries.

■ *They spend time with people who encourage their nonconformity.* It is a rare gift to find people who are loyal and protect you and give you space to be yourself. You learn to value them highly and to give them the same space they give you. I am blessed to have a wife who allows me my eccentricities. At times we operate in our individual spheres, seeing different friends, pursuing different goals. But the joy is to come together in the evenings, share our different days, and be loved without having to change or pretend to be something other than what we are.

It is the same with Mark Svensson, with whom I have had lunch once a week for 18 years. From one perspective we have little in common: he is older than I, and an immigrant from Sweden. I have spent half my life going to school, he has not bothered much with formal education. He loves opera, and I do not. Yet I eagerly look forward to our meetings because time has shown that Mark will allow me to be free with him.

Some days I am euphoric over the writing I am doing. At other times I want to spout off and complain about all the things that are going wrong and all the people who seem dedicated to doing me in. He may not like everything he sees in me, but I know that he will not bolt from the friendship because he disapproves of something. In part that is because he is something of a nonconformist himself.

■ *They are always creating something.* There is another way to develop your individuality—to carve out time for creative enterprises. Erik Erikson talked about the need, when we get older, to fight off stagnation with what he called "generativity." During some phases of our lives that need for generativity may be filled by bearing and rearing children, but when we have no children, or when children leave the nest, the need for creativity lingers.

Good therapists urge their clients to make as much contact with art and music as possible, and to do more than look and listen. They should paint, draw, sculpt, sing. Someone once said that what our country needed was more poor music. By that he meant that we need more music in the home, created on the spot, for the sheer fun of it.

▪ *They stray off the beaten path.* "Don't keep forever on the public road," Alexander Graham Bell once said. "Leave the beaten track occasionally and dive into the woods. You will be certain to find something that you've never seen before."

John Huston Finley was an individualist who quite literally got off the beaten path. His versatility was remarkable. A teacher at Princeton, a college president at Knox College and the College of the City of New York, a commissioner of education in New York State, and an editor at *The New York Times,* he was greatly admired for his walking. For example, every year on his birthday, he stuck a blue thistle in his lapel, threw a plaid scarf about his neck, and made off, hatless and coatless, on a jaunty loop around Manhattan Island before appearing at his *Times* office to put in a day's work. It is reported that one day a walk he took measured 72 miles. More than once, he walked from New York to Princeton.

▪ *They like to be with children.* Children are naturally nonconformists, "trailing clouds of glory" according to Wordsworth. Jesus doubtless had many reasons for suggesting that we become as little children,

.

but surely one of them was that they can help us think less about other people's opinions and be more spontaneous. When Theodore Roosevelt and his family were in residence at Sagamore Hill, it was always a boistrous party. One day he took his four children on an all-day picnic. The day was warm, but the children had no bathing suits. Roosevelt permitted them to go wading and soon, of course, he was swimming in his clothes with them. As he and his children came into the house, dripping water on the carpets and filling the rooms with their shouts, Mrs. Roosevelt was heard to remark: "I really have *five* boys."

▪ *They often have flair.* If we are true to our instincts, most of us will find that we naturally develop certain trademarks. Pat Kennedy recalls this about her mother Rose: "I remember Mother's good-night kiss when she'd go out with Daddy. My room was dark, and this vision just sort of appeared, smelling absolutely marvelous. I was fascinated by her perfume—we all were—and as we girls grew older, we'd ask her what it was. But she wouldn't tell us. Finally, when she was 75, she told us. Now we all wear it; it's our favorite perfume. But when we all started to smell alike, Mother changed hers to something else."

Rose Kennedy has lived so long and so well in part because she knows that God did not make us to smell alike, look alike, and act alike. Each of us was created unique, and the discovery and expression of that uniqueness is one reason we are on this planet. Resisting conformity and developing some small eccentricities is one of the steps to independence and self-confidence.

CHAPTER EIGHT

The child lacks the equipment
and experience necessary
to form an accurate picture of himself,
so his only guide
is the reactions of others to him.
There is very little cause for him
to question these appraisals,
and in any case he is far too helpless
to challenge them or to rebel against them.

—HARRY STACK SULLIVAN

Breaking Away from Parental Power

AT THE BEGINNING OF HER CAREER, Marlo Thomas wondered if people would compare her talents to those of her father, Danny Thomas. Was she as good as he was? As funny as he was? Danny set all this straight.

"You're a thoroughbred," he told his daughter right from the start, "and thoroughbreds don't watch other horses; they run their own race." Just before Marlo stepped into one of her first roles in summer stock, a package arrived in her backstage dressing room. It was a set of horse blinders and a note from her father. It said, "Run your own race, kid."

Danny Thomas was a wise father to advise his children in that fashion, for many of us were not released so freely by our parents. From this complicated set of early relationships we continue to feel waves of self-recrimination and guilt. This can occur long after our parents are gone. I am constantly amazed at how powerfully our early family experiences can continue to tug at us, even from the grave. One of my clients, who is in her seventies and has retired from a successful sales career, had to begin seeing a therapist because she dreams of her mother almost every night, and is plagued by unresolved issues with her parents. Her mother has been dead for 51 years.

The second step for living independently is:

····································

MAKE THE BEST POSSIBLE PEACE WITH YOUR PARENTS

····································

A jogger sits on a curb two miles from his home, sobbing uncontrollably. Fortunately it is late at night, and his neighbors do not see him, but it is not the first time that it has happened. In fact, he tells me, when he runs harder than usual, it is becoming an almost automatic reflex to cry.

Here is a man who, by most people's standards, is extraordinarily successful—a surgeon who spends more than half his time coaching surgical residents. He lives in a huge, two-story Tudor home with leaded glass windows and several fireplaces. He is tall and blond and slender, married to a bright, vivacious woman, and they have two children who are as good-looking and bright as they are.

At our first session it became obvious that for all this doctor's outward good fortune, he was riddled with emotional pain and plagued with self-loathing. He castigated himself for dozens of things, but I will give only one example. He told me again and again in our sessions that he did not apply himself sufficiently in medical school and should have taken better advantage of his opportunities there. This made no sense to me, since I knew that he had been asked to become a professor immediately upon completion of his residency, but no amount of arguing could change his self-criticism on this issue.

My colleague and I quickly established that this client was not psychotic. He did not hear voices and never lost touch with reality. He went to work every day and functioned in a superior manner in the outside world. He was simply mangled with overpowering fears and self-doubts. My friend's symptoms were a little more pronounced than most, but he is not unlike many people with whom I work. On the outside they seem models of confidence and success, but on the inside they are in turmoil and feel that if anyone knew them as they really are, they would react with disgust.

I asked the standard questions about traumatic experiences in the past, and he reported no more than usual. How does one go about helping such a person? It would not help to give him pep talks about how much he has to be proud of and how many reasons he should feel confident. No, old emotions from some

·

unspecified source were sweeping over him at times, like unexpected waves at the beach. Such emotions do not come from nowhere: they are almost certainly connected to some past experience or experiences too painful to be kept in the consciousness. So while the memory of the event is forgotten, the emotions linger.

As we began to work, I asked in more detail about his childhood. It seemed significant that he barely recalled the years before his parents' divorce. I asked about his parents. Were they living? Was he close to them?

"I'm fairly close to my mom. She still lives in Ohio, and I see her once or twice a year. Dad lives alone out here, but I don't see much of him. He gets on my nerves pretty quickly." Then he added hastily, "But I love him, of course—he *is* my father."

There was a slight sign of discomfort in his gestures as this topic came up, and his eyes were averted as he told me about his father. This was a possible tip-off. The following week we began hypnosis, and he proved to be an excellent subject, going under easily. And in the very first session we hit pay dirt.

It turned out that his father was hardly the lovable person he wanted to believe he had been. In fact, the man was a genuine psychotic, and the boy's childhood was one long struggle to maintain his own sanity. Until his mother finally divorced him, his father had been in and out of mental hospitals, had fits of heavy drinking, and had beaten the rest of the family regularly, sometimes when he was entirely sober.

Nearly all these early memories had been blocked from consciousness, but under hypnosis he recalled in excruciating detail times when he would hear his father beating his mother in the bedroom. "I'd lie in bed," he said, "wishing he'd come in and beat me some more because I knew I could take it and she couldn't." Some schizophrenics are gentle and loving despite their illness, but this wounded man was profoundly ill. He was paranoid, hostile, and cruel, and his two little boys were the handiest recipients of his invective.

Eventually my friend's younger brother collapsed, and he has spent most of his adult life in mental hospitals. No one knows why one child survives such hell and another does not. Somehow my client made it through. He spent as much time as possible away from the house during adolescence, and he moved away completely at the earliest opportunity. Fortunately he discovered that he had a flair for science and an ability to study long nights without sleep, and he pulled himself up to his present position by his bootstraps.

It is now much easier for both of us to understand why he originally showed up at my office talking about the recurring thought, *There's something wrong with me, and I'm no good*. Now we know something of the reason for that pumping, gushing stream of self-abuse and self-loathing despite his outward achievements, and we have discovered where he learned to talk to himself with such shame and rejection. The wonder is that he has functioned as well as he has in the outside world.

Why did the boy accept those messages from his father? Why didn't he recognize that the man was crazy and see his attacks as unwarranted? To ask a young child to weed out fiction from truth in parental messages is to ask the impossible. Toddlers do not distinguish reality from unreality; they trust the people who give them food, bathe their bodies, and help them get back to sleep when they wake up frightened at night. We have to be much older to say, "My father's got a problem and I'm going to ignore what he says here." For children to say, "My father is crazy" is in fact to go crazy themselves, so instead they decide, "There must be something wrong with me. I can't seem to do anything right." It becomes a part of a child's belief system. But the emotion hurts and is so powerful that the whole thing is stuffed into the unconscious. So it was that long periods of my patient's childhood had been blacked out.

But emotions are not as susceptible to repression as the memories that prompted them, and since the unconscious is a permanent repository, from time to time in this boy's life (for instance, when he had jogged a hard three miles and was panting) those emotions would spring up into consciousness, and a seemingly successful man found himself sitting on a curb crying.

It happens that this story has a happy ending. In several years of therapy my friend took a long look at all those repressed experiences, processed them, and began to sort out the beliefs he had brought from childhood that were no longer valid. And concomitantly, the feelings began to lose their hold on him. He no longer needs regular treatment, and the surges of self-doubt now come very rarely.

The point of the story is this: we continue to carry with us emotions of worthlessness long after the facts have changed. As a line from T. S. Eliot has it, we are "a set of obsolete responses." Thus there is value in going back over the data of our preadult years and examining the standards by which we learned to judge ourselves.

Many people who read a case such as the one reported above will say, "Well, I'm not going to go back and open up a can of worms from my past. Besides, what good does it do to blame your parents for everything?" This is a fair question and reflects a common criticism of psychotherapy. Most therapists do not pursue the past in order to blame other people for their client's problems. Most parents did the best they knew how. Nor do we look back in order to find scapegoats or to escape responsibility for our problems. Quite to the contrary, we look to the past precisely in order to make some changes in our course. Only with some insight as to how we arrived at our present position can we take measures to change our direction. Insight may not solve the problem, but it is the first step.

Forgiving Our Parents

The next step, if we discover that our parents got us off to a bad start, is to forgive them. First, it may be necessary to relive the anguish and feel the anger. It would have been fruitless to advise my surgeon friend to forgive his father when he did not even remember the experiences or feel the anger. And in some cases, we need some time to be angry. But it is folly to spend the rest of our lives raging against unfair parents, for it poisons our psychological system and can be like an acid that slops out on all our relationships. It is possible to say to ourselves, *My parents were wrong to have put me down, and I am now correcting the standards by which I was judged as a child, but I refuse to carry resentment against anyone for the rest of my life.*

Some people who have laid to rest some resentment from the past and have finally been able to forgive an authority who wronged them will say, "I finally have peace, but I'm worried that it won't last. I'm afraid my anger will come back."

Since all of our relationships vacillate, and since our internal emotions also have great variation, it is indeed quite likely that their resentment will return. Does this mean that the experience of forgiveness was invalid? Not at all. When Jesus said we were to forgive 70 times 7 times, I suspect that he had precisely such relationships in mind. They are not laid to rest with one act. We will find ourselves forgiving again and again, in the same manner that God forgives us.

A caveat may be in order here, though. Deciding to forgive our parents does not mean that we will like them and will want to spend a lot of time with them. It simply means that we choose to forgive them.

Most of us have not had the childhood traumas described above, and we find ourselves with bundles of both love and resentment toward our early families. Let's say that you looked up to your older brother and would have done anything to gain his favor, but he was constantly making fun of you as you tried to keep up, and you have always felt inferior. Or suppose that you love your parents and always look forward to visiting them, but when you're with them it's never as good as you expect it to be. Somehow they make you feel like you are still a small child. Such are the ambivalences that nearly all of us have with our families.

Accepting Limitations in Our Relationships

Occasionally, no matter how hard we try, no matter how often we go back, we simply do not find what we're looking for in our parents or our siblings. They may be too troubled, too angry, too selfish, or too manipulative, and simply incapable of the love we long to receive.

The surgeon I spoke of earlier came to that conclusion about his father during therapy. He returned home twice, trying to establish some beachhead. But he failed. "It hurts to say it," he told me, "but I'm obviously not going to get anything from that man, so I'm going to stop trying." There was a tear in his eye, and he paused. Then he said, "It's funny how much release I feel in just saying that. I'm not going to get any love from him, so I don't have to go back and get kicked any more."

Reconciliation

On the other hand, many of us can resolve a great deal with our parents long after we become adults. Dr. Harold H. Bloomfield tells about his father's final bout with cancer. They had lived 3000 miles apart, and Bloomfield would drop in to see his parents when in New York, but the visits were limited to an hour or two. "By holding a tight lid on my conflicting feelings for them, I always managed to avoid a confrontation during our strained conversations," he says. "I resented my father for always being the martyr and for arguing so passionately with my mother, so I stayed away."

But when Bloomfield walked into the hospital room, his father's skin was jaundiced and he had lost 30 pounds. A few days later, when his father was sitting up in bed, Bloomfield said,

"Dad, I really feel for what's happened to you. It's helped me to look at the ways I've kept my distance and to feel how much I really love you." I leaned over and started to give him a hug, but his shoulders and arms tensed up.

"C'mon, Dad, I really want to give you a hug."

For a moment he looked shocked. Showing affection was not our usual way of relating. When he tensed up I could feel the resentment starting to build inside me, and I was almost ready to say something like "I don't *need* this. If you want to leave me with the same coldness as always, go right ahead." For years I had used every instance of my father's resistance to say to myself, "See, he doesn't care." This time, however, I thought again and realized the hug was for *my* benefit as well as my father's.

I leaned up close to him at the edge of the bed with his arms around me. "Now squeeze. That's it. Now again, squeeze. Very good!"

In a sense I was showing my father how to hug, and as he squeezed, something happened. For an instant, a feeling of "I love you" sneaked through.

It was up to me to be the source of many, many hugs before my father died. I was not blaming him; after all, he was changing the habits of an entire lifetime—and that takes time. I knew we were succeeding because more and more we were relating out of care and affection. Around the two-hundredth hug, he spontaneously said out loud, for the first time I could ever recall, "I love you."*

Bloomfield's father, who had been given less than six months to live, had four high-quality years. "Those four years of peace with my parents made a tremendous difference in my life," he writes. "With a new . . . model of love and commitment in my mind, I was able to break through my fears and share more love in my marriage. I also gained inner peace."

Such a full, peaceful reconciliation with the key figures of one's past will not be achievable for everyone, but when it happens, it is wonderful. And the rule is an important one: Make the best possible peace with your parents.

---

* From the book *Making Peace with Your Parents*, by Harold H. Bloomfield, M.D., published by Ballantine books, © 1983 Bloomfield Productions.

PART
FOUR

DEALING WITH THE ENEMIES OF SELF-CONFIDENCE

CONFIDENCE
. . . .
CHAPTER NINE

By both precept and example
George had been taught to regard his body
as something he should master,
subdue, and order about.

—H. A. WILLIAMS

Clearing
the Confusion
about Your Body

MOST OF US CONTINUE to have a great deal of confusion as adults about our bodies and thus about ourselves. For one thing, we seem to have considerable confusion as to what our bodies actually look like. In 1985, *Psychology Today* surveyed 30,000 people about body image. The study was designed by psychologist Thomas F. Cash, and others, who made interesting comparisons with a similar survey taken 13 years earlier. In 1972, 15% of the men and 25% of the women were dissatisfied with their overall appearance, and in 1985, 34% of the men and 38% of the women did not like their looks. Most of the dissatisfaction centered on weight. Forty-one percent of the men wanted to weigh less, and a startling 55% of the women thought they were overweight. While 20% of the respondents did not like the way their faces looked, fully 50% of the men and 57% of the women were dissatisfied with their mid-torsos. It appears that in this age of obsessive shaping up and trying to look good, we are nevertheless more and more dissatisfied with ourselves.

But to compound the problem, we evidently see our bodies as being considerably less attractive than they actually are. It has long been noted that persons suffering from eating disorders such as bulimia and anorexia have misshapen ideas of what they look like, but in a recent piece of research, J. Kevin Thompson studied the attitudes of more than 100 women who were free of such disorders. He found that more than 95% overestimated their body size—on average they thought they were one-fourth larger than they really were. When asked to adjust light beams on the wall in four spaces to show the width of their cheeks, waist, hips, and thighs, the researchers found that two women in five estimated at least one body part to be 50% larger than it actually was.

Perhaps the most important finding by Dr. Cash was this: "There is little connection between how attractive people are and how attractive they feel they are, particularly among women. A woman who seems quite unattractive can be quite content with her body, while another who is highly attractive can be so obsessed with every little flaw in her appearance that she feels ugly."

The Inside-Outside Controversy

There is also confusion as to how we *should* feel about these bodies of ours. As one 36-year-old woman wrote, "I've always known I was attractive, and I think it has made life easier for me, but I have never gotten over feeling a little guilty about being proud of the way I look."

Her guilt was perhaps created by the bromide we have heard over and over: "Honey, it's not what's on the outside that counts, but what's on the inside." In fact, many Christian thinkers argue that what's on the outside does not count at all and should be ignored, if not directly fought.

Such a cogent thinker as C. S. Lewis fails us on this point. "The fact that we have bodies," he said, "is the oldest joke there is." He inveighed against the "Neo-Pagans . . . , the nudists and the sufferers from Dark Gods, to whom the body is glorious," and opted instead for the view of St. Francis, who saw his body as "Brother Ass."

"Ass," says Lewis, "is exquisitely right because no one in his senses can either revere or hate a donkey. It is a useful, sturdy, lazy, obstinate, patient, lovable and infuriating beast; deserving now the stick and now a carrot; both pathetically and absurdly beautiful. So the body. There's no living with it till we recognize that one of its functions in our lives is to play the part of the buffoon."

There is some justification for Lewis's view. A part of us *does* transcend the body, and we will live after our bodies die and decay. But the New Testament clearly teaches the doctrine of the resurrection of the *body*, and none of us is able to live well on this planet by treating our physical existence as if it were inconsequential.

Integration of Body and Spirit

We have a strong allegiance to and identification with our bodies. In a rich but little-known book, *True Resurrection*, H. A. Williams argues that the dualism between body and mind must be transcended. For him, some of the import of the resurrection is, "mind and body no longer making war on each other in a bid for domination, but recognizing that they are both equally me." The body is not all we are, and the time will come when we will exist without this present body, but God has created us as physical beings, which is to say that my body is myself, not a machine I own. To help overcome a major obstacle to self-confidence, the rule is:

....

DETERMINE TO INTEGRATE THE BODY AND SPIRIT
....

Such an integration entails several steps:

Step 1: Keep Your Flaws in Perspective

We will, for instance, refuse to get obsessed with our flaws. Journalist Cynthia Gorney tells about her struggle with fat thighs:

They didn't pop out and devastate me until I was around thirteen when, of course, it mattered so desperately not to have them. But before I was born, they were set in the genes, some nasty generations-old legacy of a hard-working peasant back in Poland who never knew how much I would hate them.

Here is how I found out they ran in the family: It was midsummer and I was out by a swimming pool, wrapped up tight in a terry-cloth robe. I had charted the distance between my chaise lounge and the water. I knew that if I dropped the robe at precisely the right moment I could dash to the edge of the pool and be submerged before anybody saw. I dropped the robe. My aunt, a charming person with a voice you could hear across a football field, looked as I dashed. "Oh, my," my aunt said. "She's certainly got the family thighs."

I am a nice-looking person. I have blue eyes, decent hair, not too many pimples, and long eyelashes that have been known to stir mild envy now and then. None of this matters. I could have a face like Miss Universe, and it would not matter. The only thing that has ever mattered to me, when I take off my clothes and look in the mirror, is my great big terrible lumpy thighs.

Such obsessions with physical failings are very common. Lauren Hutton says her nose is uneven; Linda Ronstadt thinks she "looks awful in photographs"; Suzanne Somers thinks her legs are too thin; Jayne Kennedy thought she was too tall when she was young; Kristy McNichol thinks her lips are too fat.

When a person has obvious physical flaws, there are two things to do. The first is to figure out whether you can reasonably do anything about it, and the second is to act on those findings. If there are no corrective steps possible (for instance, you can do little about your height), then you can simply put the matter out of your mind and go on to thinking about other, more important things. But if exercise will help, then by all means you should exercise. If corrective surgery is reasonable, then perhaps you should do it. But be fore-warned that plastic surgeons have been telling us for a long time that when people are obsessed with their noses and get them fixed, it usually does little to en-hance their self-images. They simply move on to an obsession with another part of their anatomy that they wish were different. Our obsession with our body parts is often a symptom rather than a cause. It is a symptom of general low self-image and of habitually assaulting our inner selves with negative material.

Step 2: Avoid Needless Comparisons

Part of our difficulty with body image is the problem of comparison. We are constantly comparing ourselves with those being admired or criticized. As one woman said, "Once the scale hits 160 pounds, life's greatest pleasure is seeing some woman who is heavier than you are." This habit of comparing ourselves with oth-ers is exceedingly dangerous, especially if we compare ourselves with the youthful examples of perfection to be found on the TV screen. When one is walking through a crowd of people, say, in an airline terminal, it can be rather startling how few of the persons there look anything like those who populate the commercials for beauty products on TV. Instead, one is struck with how average they look.

The biblical emphasis is that our bodies have worth and are made by God, and that they were made to be used wisely. Whether they look impressive or not is much less important than what we do with them. When Samuel was sent out to choose a king from the sons of Jesse, this is what the Lord said to him: "Do not consider his appearance or his height. . . . The Lord does not look at the things man looks at. Man looks at the outward appearance, but the Lord looks at the heart" (1 Sam. 16:7).

Gail MacDonald, an acquaintance whom I know to be eminently attractive, commented on a magazine advertisement featuring the photo of a model whose "enviable growth of blond hair . . . suggests that beauty is found in a bottle of hair conditioner. What woman doesn't desire the beauty that makes people notice and admire her?"

But MacDonald does not regard herself as having ideal looks:

Frankly, my view of my self has not always been a healthy one. As a teenager I remember the strong surges of inner frustration over unending battles with pimples, embarrassment over what I deemed an unsightly nose and a front tooth which should have received dental correction but didn't. As a result of my sensitivity, I often felt uneasy in crowds. I was certain that the facial blemishes, the nose, and the tooth were all that anyone ever noticed about me.

It was no easy task, and it did not happen quickly, but I was able to overcome those feelings when, as a Christian woman, I realized that people could be drawn to the quality of my spirit rather than to the shape of my face.

At times I considered the words of Paul (who apparently was not much to look at either): "I can do all things through Christ which strengtheneth me."

It worked! Yes, it was a long process, but it worked. I finally came to realize that I was truly God's daughter [and] . . . my "self-image" began to change dramatically. I still think my nose is too big, and I occasionally have to cover up a pimple. The tooth in the front of my mouth still crosses its neighbor just a bit, but I hardly care. I've attempted to enhance "beauty" from another source. . . . A woman makes an enormous leap forward in her spiritual development when she determines that being *useful* is more important than being *noticed*.

Step 3: Cultivate the Senses

We need to chart a middle course between the hedonists who obey every impulse of the body and the ascetics who believe that if you punish the body you achieve a higher state. Our bodies are indeed ourselves, and the imperfections with which we are born are inconsequential compared to the good things our bodies can do for us.

We have a great deal of control over those things. We can decide, for instance, how well we pay attention to the constant sensations coming into us. And the better we pay attention, the better we are going to feel about our bodies, for they are marvelously sensitive webs of interconnected, sensation-receiving abilities.

The Duke in Shakespeare's play *As You Like It* is

abruptly removed from the pleasures of the palace, and his band of men has to try to survive in the forest with too few blankets. But this is what he says:

> Here feel we but the penalty of Adam,
> The seasons' difference; as, the icy fang
> And churlish chiding of the winter's wind,
> Which, when it bites and blows upon my body
> Even till I shrink with cold, I smile, and say
> "This is no flattery; these are counselors
> That feelingly persuade me what I am."

The Duke is right: there is something about receiving even such elemental sensations as hot and cold that "feelingly persuade" us that we *are*, and we need to be open to all the good that comes through our senses.

May Fenn tells of attending a Braille-reading competition many years ago that was being held in the presence of Elizabeth, the Queen Mother. Her attention was caught by a little blind girl who was holding the bouquet of flowers to be presented to Elizabeth. As she waited, the child gently ran her fingers over every bloom before breathing in its perfume. Later, Fenn glanced at the Queen Mother and was surprised to see that her eyes were closed. Just as the blind girl had done, she was letting her fingers feel the flowers she had been given. She, too, had noticed and was trying to experience the beauty of flowers through the sense of touch.

Step 4: Use Your Body to Give Love

We will feel better about ourselves the more we give ourselves away, and that principle applies to our bodies as much as to the rest of us. Much of the information other people gather about themselves has to do with the physical contact they receive from us. Young children come to have certain perceptions of themselves in part from the way their bodies are handled by those of us who care for them. If mother and father, when giving you a bath, seem to like who you are and the body you own, that is imparted by the way they touch. And it is imparted by the way they react when your body is cut or bruised.

Later, this body contact is often withdrawn. When a child is older, parents stop touching so much, and often the message is that your body has grown in such ways that you're no longer attractive. Again and again in my practice I talk to teenage girls who cannot understand why their fathers stopped hugging them when they developed breasts.

Later in life, much data about ourselves comes from our mates, and there can be few experiences in life that leave you feeling so good about who you are as the joy of gradual arousal to a peak connection with the one you love. But good sex must be more than recreational diversion; it must be communication. And part of what a husband and wife communicate in bed is this: I admire and value the person you are.

But how important is sex, and what happens if you are not married or are incapacitated sexually? That need not diminish your ability to affirm another. Ann Landers once published an anguished letter from a man who feared that the woman he loved was deprived because a physical condition prevented him from completing the sex act. In response, Landers received the following comment from an Oregon woman:

That man is totally ignorant of the workings of the female mind and heart. If you were to ask 100 women how they feel about sexual intercourse, I'll bet 98 would say "Just hold me close and be tender. Forget the rest." If you don't believe it, why not take a poll? People tell you things they would never tell anyone else.

"You're on," Ann Landers wrote back, then asked her women readers to reply to the question, "Would you be content to be held close and treated tenderly and forget about 'the act?' Answer YES or NO and please add one line: 'I am over (or under) 40 years of age.' "

Within four days the mailroom was working double shifts and weekends to handle the replies. She had obviously struck a nerve. Over 100,000 replies poured in. The results: 72% of the respondents said yes, they would be content just to be held close and treated tenderly and forget about the sex act. Of those 72%, 40% were under 40 years of age. Obviously the sexual revolution has not provided much help to the average person who says, "I want to be valued. I want to feel cared about." Tender words and loving embraces are more rewarding than an orgasm produced by a silent, mechanical, self-involved partner.

The Aging Body

Many of the clients I see are over 60. Often they are depressed because of the deterioration of their bodies, and they have become negative toward themselves.

If they are physically ill and their once-strong bodies are not cooperating, it can prompt self-loathing. Such persons need physical contact more than ever. Where ever did we get the idea that because people are infirm or confined to nursing homes and no longer have sexual intercourse that they no longer need touching and physical affirmation?

A woman tells about the weeks when her 80-year-old father was dying of cancer. Their relationship had at times been strained, but now they seemed to want to be with each other, and she was in his room for hours every day. "I didn't always know what to say to him as he suffered there," she said, "so I spent a lot of time massaging his feet."

That said a great deal. At some primal level, when we touch another we say, "You are lovable still, you are valid, you are *there*."

Step 5: Keep Your Body Finely Tuned

Since physical health determines to a great extent one's general happiness, it makes sense to treat our bodies well. Although we cannot prove which causes which, people with good self-images tend to eat better and exercise more than those with low self-confidence. I am not a medical doctor, but I often ask depressed patients what they've eaten in the last 24 hours and about their exercise habits. The way they are taking care of themselves is one of the best tip-offs as to the state of their self-images.

An astonishing number of us abuse our bodies with

an almost self-destructive bent, and we eat so poorly and exercise so negligently that our bodies are giving us all sorts of sluggish sensations, headaches, pains, and general lassitude. We cannot feel very positive about ourselves with all that going on. Despite the fitness boom, a recent study by the U.S. Department of Health and Human Services shows that 80% to 90% of us do not get enough exercise. Almost a third of American men and more than a third of women are obese—just as they were a decade ago.

And keeping your body fit enough to make you feel good does not require that much. Kenneth Cooper, the doctor who coined and popularized the term *aerobics*, now says that walking three miles in 45 minutes, five times a week is all the aerobics conditioning anybody needs. Exercise more than that, he said recently, and "you are running for something other than fitness." Various studies have shown that working out is good for blood-sugar control, sexual performance, the immune system, the circulatory system, breaking down blood clots, losing weight, gaining muscle, reducing stress, and alleviating depression.

So the way you treat your body, the way you keep it smoothly functioning, will interconnect with the way you feel about yourself.

Is Fat Lovable?

Having said all the above, I must comment on the possibility of being ungainly and still maintaining an excellent self-image. A young college man I know, who could have attracted almost any woman on campus, enjoyed dating an overweight girl, and this is what he said about her: "The thing that impressed me when I met her was that she was fat and talked freely about it and didn't seem to let it worry her. She's the most loving, enjoyable woman I've known, and best of all, she feels good about herself. Most of the girls I've dated who looked like models are forever groaning about gaining too much weight, kicking themselves for eating too much and telling me that there are all sorts of things they don't like about their bodies."

So the trick is either to change our bodies or to accept them as they are. To fail to do anything to change them and at the same time castigate our looks diminishes our confidence. If you are overweight, for example, you have two options: either get on a diet and exercise program, or say, "For right now I'm going to be a little fat and I'm going to enjoy living, including everything I eat." We must reject the third option, which is to do nothing about our weight but to drive along the freeway every day saying, "I'm so fat. I've got to do something about this. Why can't I use self-discipline? I'm so ugly."

Perhaps the healthy view of one's body is best illustrated by a churchman, now in his early eighties, who has stayed in excellent physical condition, and who occasionally goes alone to his mountain cabin to pray and study. "The place is very private," he says, "so I often strip naked and enjoy the freedom of moving about the house unencumbered and free." There is not a drop of narcissism in this man, and his spirituality and disciplined devotional life are admirable.

I see his attitude as an integration of body and spirit. His model reminds us that we need to become more attuned to our bodies' sensations, remembering that we do not *have* bodies, we *are* bodies.

CONFIDENCE

. . . .

CHAPTER TEN

*Conscience takes up more room than
all the rest of a person's insides.*

—HUCKLEBERRY FINN

Shedding
the Albatross
of Unearned Guilt

SINCE ALL OF THE THERAPISTS at our clinic are
Christians, we see many very religious people, and a
lot of them are excessively hard on themselves.
Depression is often a part of the syndrome. Though
some of these clients may be quite successful and appear to have everything going for them, they are riddled with guilt.

When we become believers we do not automatically
shed our neuroses. As a woman told Dr. Cecil Osborne
during group therapy, "I used to be a terrible neurotic.
Then I was converted, and now I'm a *Christian* neurotic!"

She laughed, and the others joined in. They understood all too well that becoming a Christian does not
instantly cure one's problems. In fact, one could make

a case that as our faith increases, the more sensitive our consciences become, and the more negative our self-estimates. But that would be an oversimplification, and a misunderstanding of the difference between true faith and sick religion. Religion is sick if it pushes people down, makes them feel bad about themselves without relief, and urges them to punish themselves regularly. The aim of healthy faith is to distinguish between false guilt and genuine guilt, then help a person expiate that guilt rather than wallow in it. The main purpose of this chapter is to distinguish between these two approaches, and our rule is:

····································

DETERMINE TO LIVE ABOVE NEUROTIC GUILT

····································

In talking about release from guilt, we first need to distinguish guilt from its emotional cousin, shame. In his book *Feelings,* Willard Gaylin is quite helpful here. Shame, he demonstrates, has more to do with public exposure than guilt. You can feel ashamed when you're pulled over by a police officer and sit while waiting for your ticket, as people drive by with a mixture of amusement and ridicule. But you can also have shame when you show up at a party that was announced as formal and you are wearing casual clothes. So shame and embarrassment have to do with public ridicule, which we all want to avoid, but may or may not be connected to any wrongdoing on our part. In the case of the party, we merely feel foolish, and in the case of the speeding ticket, we may or may not feel guilty.

Most of us engage in a certain amount of behavior that we do not consider wrong, but which, if exposed, would elicit disapproval from certain people and actual punishment from others. In the latter case it is the hand-in-the-cookie-jar scenario that we try to avoid. We disagree with the standard by which we are being judged (for example, we were exceeding the speed limit, but we think the limit was too low), but we will go to great lengths to avoid punishment.

Shame has much of the same emotional content as guilt, but it is not the same thing. It is the clutching sensation we experience when we are speeding down the freeway and hear the wail of a siren. We do not like the idea of another person scolding us, we do not like the embarrassment of sitting there while the ticket is being written, we do not like the sensation of having been stupid enough to get caught, and we don't like the prospect of paying the fine. But this bundle of emotions may still not include guilt. Here is Willard Gaylin's way of testing it: If you hear the siren, clutch up, then see the officer passing you in order to pull over the Porsche that passed you a few minutes ago, and all the negative emotions evaporate—what you were feeling was fear rather than guilt. If you feel bad for having exceeded the speed limit, and even some disappointment that you didn't get apprehended, then indeed what you have is true guilt.

Healthy Guilt and Neurotic Guilt

Genuine guilt is connected to wrongs we have done or good things we have left undone and, contrary to certain pop psychologists who call such feelings "the unnecessary emotions," they in fact keep society glued together. Martin Buber said that the most poignant guilt stems from some violation of human relationships, that causes us to say to ourselves, "How could I have done that to him?" But there is also what Stanford psychiatrist Irvin D. Yalom refers to as existential guilt: "a positive, constructive emotion—a perception of the difference between what a thing is and what it ought to be." Christians see this as guilt arising from a violation of God's commands, and sometimes it has nothing to do with other persons. Sometimes it is a thing no one knows about and will never know about. Yet it is wrong.

Analyst Selma Fraiberg writes that a healthy conscience produces guilt feelings commensurate with the act and that guilt feelings serve to prevent our repeating such acts. "But the neurotic conscience," she writes, "behaves like a gestapo headquarters within the personality, mercilessly tracking down dangerous or potentially dangerous ideas and every remote relative of these ideas, accusing, threatening, tormenting in an interminable inquisition to establish guilt for trivial offenses or crimes committed in dreams. Such guilt feelings have the effect of putting the whole personality under arrest."

Judith Viorst is not quite so theoretical:

I feel guilty whenever my children are unhappy.
I feel guilty whenever I fail to floss after eating.
I feel guilty whenever I step on a bug deliberately—
all cockroaches excepted.

I feel guilty whenever I cook with a pat of butter that I have dropped on the kitchen floor.

And because, if there were room, I could easily list several hundred more of such genuinely guilt-provoking items, I would say that I am suffering from an excessive, indiscriminate sense of guilt.

The Pleasure of Punishment

Dr. Lars Granberg once said, "Show me what you read most in the Bible and I can tell you worlds about yourself," and it is interesting to see how some people are drawn again and again to the imprecatory psalms and to the condemning passages in the Bible. Secularists castigate Christians for their obsession with sin, guilt, and self-flagellation. But one reason for the excessive self-flagellation among certain people is that they have the mistaken idea that they are holiest when they are most critical of themselves, that God is most pleased by the humble, self-effacing pilgrim who is constantly asking forgiveness. Guilt somehow becomes a badge of devotion.

But the habit of apologizing at such length is misguided and unhealthy. When prayer consists only of people detailing to God all the wrongs they have done and all the good they have left undone, it is a perversion of the great idea of grace in the Scriptures.

Suppose that I have lunch with a friend regularly, and I take most of that time to reiterate how terrible I am and how far I have fallen short of the way I ought to live. The friend would soon find excuses for canceling our lunch engagements. It is not pleasant to be around people who are forever running themselves down, forever apologizing. The message is, "Pardon me for existing," and it is not the way God intended us to live.

Guilt as Escape

Considerable psychological research has been done on guilt as a means of getting some secondary gain. It can, for instance, be little more than a bid for attention. It can be a way of saying, "Note how highly developed my conscience is." Or, "Don't think I'm doing this out of stupidity—I'm quite aware that it's wrong." Oliver Wendell Holmes said, "Apologizing is a very desperate habit—one that is rarely cured. Apology is only egotism wrong side out. Nine times out of ten, the first thing a man's companion knows of his shortcomings is from his apology. It is mighty presumptuous on your part to suppose your small failure of so much consequence that you must talk about it."

Much more serious is guilt as a way of avoiding responsibility. The trouble with excessive guilt, self-flagellation, and constant apologizing is that it does not make you more guarded or more bent toward changing. Instead, it paralyzes you. If you feel bad enough about yourself you do not have to change—you're not up to it. It is a short distance from saying, "I am a terrible sinner" to saying, "poor me."

Skeletons in the Closet

For many persons, the memories of past failures are constantly before them and they spend a lot of emotional energy keeping those failures hidden from others. A woman who had an abortion as a teenager and has now been happily married for many years may walk in fear that her husband will find out. Or a man may have been divorced many years ago and none of his present friends know about it. Or some spectacular failure has been covered up. Insecure persons will try hard to keep such secrets hidden and may cover their tracks with lies and obfuscations. The result is a life of duplicity and a very tense, controlled person who lacks freedom and creativity. Creativity implies a certain amount of freedom of expression, abandon, a refusal to worry about what other people are thinking, an ability to laugh at oneself. And for those qualities to grow, one must have a relaxed connection to the memory of one's failures.

Everyone has skeletons in the closet. And the worst thing about them is the effect they have on us each time we walk down the corridor that passes the closet. Pulses quicken, breathing is tense and quick, and we want to race past the locked door. In psychotherapy, we urge clients to unlock the closet and stare the skeleton down. The first time you try it, it will nearly do you in. The second time will not be quite so hard. And if you open the door enough times, you become so accustomed to its existence that you can walk down the hallway unaffected.

I am not saying that you should open the door and exhibit your skeletons to every guest who comes to your door. There is no necessity for parading your failures to everyone, or even to feel that you must reveal everything about yourself to people who ask. We all have a right to privacy. But it is one thing to choose when and to whom you will reveal certain negative things about yourself, and quite another to be scrambling through life trying to keep everyone from knowing anything dark about yourself. That is not ordinary guilt; that is shame. It's the wrongheaded belief that you have a more embarrassing past than other people, and that they would be shocked to know how badly you have stumbled.

What is involved here is reckoning with your past, being able to accept the fact that you have erred, and even discussing your mistakes with certain people. Several things can happen when we confess our faults to another. One is clarification. One woman with rather weak ego strength was for a few months sucked into the orbit of a very powerful woman who made a prostitute of her. The experience was brief and was followed by almost 20 years of virtual celibacy. She is a devout Catholic and says there is no doubt in her mind that she has been forgiven. Why, then, does she need to discuss it with me at length? Because she still does not understand how it happened and is obviously confused as to which person is the real self—that young woman who dutifully worked as a prostitute 20 years ago, or the severely chaste woman she now is. The answer probably is that neither of these is her central self, but she needs time to talk about these two selves, to look at them in different lights, to be asked questions about them, and to have the opportunity to clarify her thinking about herself.

Catharsis is another powerful result of confession. Over and over people will say to their pastor or therapist, "I'm saying things to you I've never spoken to another human being," and it is obvious afterward that it has been like lancing an infection. The relief is enormous.

A third result is that if the hearer is not horrified at the revelation and continues to value you, it helps you to accept yourself. In the case of the woman who had briefly been a prostitute, she feared that when she told me this news I would be disgusted and stop seeing her for therapy. Of course that did not happen. I was touched by her revelation and saddened that she had somehow felt she should live a life without love and marriage in order to compensate for her sin. My acceptance of her was, I believe, at least some small aid in helping her accept herself.

The false optimists try to smile and sweep their pasts under the rug. That is not the biblical approach at all. The Bible freely acknowledges suffering and failure and personal disgrace. All the great saints of the Bible had spotted records. The Bible does not try to disguise that. So the closer we are to the Bible, the freer we should be about acknowledging our faults.

The question is not whether you have avoided failure in the past. No one who has attempted anything of consequence has avoided failure. The questions rather are: What do you do with your failures? And have those experiences caused you to doubt your abilities from that time on? Or because of the pain and embarrassment of the failure, do you try to avoid any hint of vulnerability in the future, and become, then, a self-doubting, cautious, small-thinking, self-recriminating person?

Release from Guilt

The great British clergyman Leslie Weatherhead once wrote, "The forgiveness of God is the most powerful therapeutic idea in the world. If a person can really believe that God has forgiven him, he can be saved from neuroticism." Although he has perhaps overstated the case, we do have available such a complete expiation of sins that we should confess our sins to God regularly, and such practices can greatly enhance mental health.

The problem for many of us is this: we confess our faults to God, ask for forgiveness, and then, as we get to our feet, rather than leaving the bundle of our faults there with God, we hoist it back to our shoulders and stagger back out the door carrying the same burdens. The Bible is quite clear about forgiveness being discovery as well as action: we learn that we can live fully in the present and put the past behind us. Paul said, "One thing I do: forgetting what is behind and straining toward what is ahead, I press on" (Phil. 3:13-14). Eleanor Roosevelt, when asked how she managed to accomplish so much, replied, "I don't waste time on regrets."

Why then do we walk about feeling so much remorse and self-recrimination? In large part it is due to simple habit. If we are in a family where we are constantly put down, we must strike an arrangement with our family members whereby they stop doing that. If we go to a church where the minister motivates with fear and guilt, it may mean that we should find another environment, and change to a church where the love and grace of God are properly emphasized. (Motivation by guilt, incidentally, is the lazy way to motivate our children or our parishioners, but it is very, very effective. If we make children feel guilty because they have hurt us and made us sad, they will do anything for us. If we pout a lot, we can control them like puppets.)

A young engineer with whom I worked for some time had discovered many of the origins of his self-doubt, but without getting much relief from his excessive self-hatred. One day he related a dream he had had, after which he said he realized that he had "an automatic critic" within him. It was, he said, almost as if this critic were a person inside him, whispering negative, guilt-producing messages in his ear every time he wanted to attempt something significant. He decided to create another voice within himself, answering the critic's false charges. He was able to recognize the times when the critic was speaking, because he always had tension in his shoulders when he was thinking such self-critical thoughts. So he worked on developing an alter-ego to talk back to this critical voice, and he reported astonishing relaxation and freedom that came from the exercise.

It is also possible to "rotate" certain beliefs we have about ourselves. A friend who is the soul of conscientiousness had a great deal of trouble with a rebellious son, and he was very hard on himself because his son turned out so poorly. This self-criticism was so bad that he was losing weight and couldn't sleep. Finally, he went to a therapist who subscribed to the rational-emotive school of thought. After two sessions the therapist said, "I hear you making the following statements of belief:

1. My son does not want to communicate with me.
2. I have done something to make Curt this way, and he won't tell me what it is.

3. Backpacking, UCLA football games, and all the shared things have suddenly gone out the window, forever.

4. I have so much hurt and it is not going to go away.

My friend was startled to have his belief system so well summarized by the therapist after only two sessions, and agreed that indeed those were things he said to himself over and over. The therapist suggested that he say the following things to himself, if he could indeed believe them. (Note that they were not changed into overly positive approaches to the situation—that would have been a violation of what my friend knew to be true. But they were rotated to much more hopeful statements):

1. My son and I have been having a lot of trouble communicating, but maybe we can learn a better way.

2. Curt has chosen to be this way, and Joan and I have contributed a little. He cannot tell me what it is we have done because it is in his unconscious.

3. Some precious things *are* gone, but they can and must be replaced.

4. I have so much hurt; I certainly do want to get rid of it, and there are ways to do so.

In addition to better statements of beliefs, the right sort of visualization can be of considerable help. Norman Vincent Peale suggests this:

Try visualizing a blackboard with a jumble of disconnected words and phrases, or a tangle of scrawled mathematical problems with wrong answers—in short, a sorry record of mistakes. Then image a shining figure, the Lord Himself, sweeping a sponge or a damp cloth across that blackboard, wiping it clean, preparing it for another, stronger, better effort. The Lord has forgiven your sins and mistakes. Then forgive yourself, for if you don't the old guilt circle will repeat itself. Run this total picture sequence over and over in your mind. What you are imaging is forgiveness and acceptance, and if the vision is vivid enough, a great sense of peace and well-being will follow.

Perfectionism

There is another aspect of guilt that is to be found in abundance: the tendency to feel bad every time we do something less than perfectly and to avoid any task at which we are not sure of succeeding.

Let me illustrate. A very tense, very tight man came to my office because he hated his work. He could not sleep and had been seeing his doctor for ulcers and for severe pain in his neck and lower back.

I asked about his work.

"Well, I'm a junior high school principal, and the school business is not much fun anymore. I have a very good assignment, but it's getting me down. I've never been able to take a break or stop for lunch. I eat at my desk and close the door for maybe 10 minutes. I get to work about 7:30 and leave about 6:30. And for the first six weeks of school and the last six weeks I take boxes of work home and probably put in a good 10 hours on Saturday."

I asked why he worked so hard.

"Because there's nobody else to do it. We're short on staff and there's more and more paperwork, and I can't live with myself if I don't get it done."

"Do all the principals work that many hours?" I asked.

"No, I'm sure they don't."

"Is your supervisor on your back?"

"Oh no, he's easy to work for. No, these standards are self-imposed. I do this for myself, not for anyone else. Nobody at the district office is going to know whether I leave at 4:30 or 6:00. I do it because I just can't stand to leave things undone. I just feel so guilty."

As we talked more, it became obvious to him that his perfectionistic standards were unreasonable. If he had to work 100 hours a week to get everything done, would he? Would he work 150 hours? Most of us have to learn to leave a lot of good things undone and, in fact, experts on time management tell us that the secret to living successfully is to choose only the most important things to do and to leave the insignificant things undone.

This school principal began to analyze the habits he had long ago established. He had grown up among a family of ne'er-do-wells, and in order to make his mark he had to distance himself from them and become a very self-disciplined student. At college he had no money and worked a full eight hours every day in addition to going to classes and doing homework. That meant that he could not waste a single slice of time. He so steeled himself for working hard that he learned to feel very bad about himself if he *ever* lay back and relaxed.

Such self-discipline stood him in good stead and got him to his present position. "I had a terrible self-image as a kid," he said, "but as soon as I got my college degree and became a teacher, I felt quite good about myself, quite competent." And by so pushing himself, he had gone a long way.

But now he is not driven by ambition—he can't wait to retire. He is secure among his peers, has a good position, and knows he is one of the best administrators in the city.

But he is still driven by habit—the habit of being propelled by guilt. The longer he has done it, the less clear it is why he does it, and now he is so habituated as a perfectionist that it is endangering other things that he holds dear, such as his marriage and his relationship with his children.

This man traces it back to being constantly punished and put down as a child. As punishment, he would be made to take all the dishes out of the cupboard and wash and dry them six times. He felt very low about himself. Then he became a teacher and his self-esteem began to rise, for he could see almost immediately that he was a better teacher than most. The reason was quite simple: he put in far more hours and energy than anyone else. And why did he do that? Because he was both hungry for affirmation and was succeeding at something for a change. Secondly, he still feared so many things from so many people. He had the innate fear that if he messed something up he would be scolded and condemned and covered with shame.

As this man's therapist, I am perplexed to know how much he should be helped to end his compulsive habits, for they have made him a very, very good teacher and carried him a long way. Dr. Ralph Greenson once said that if there was no such thing as neurosis, precious little would get accomplished in this world.

Yet this man's compulsion to work is excessive and he is growing in his excessiveness. Here he is, almost ready to retire, and he is still plagued by perfectionism. He has worked this way so long that he has forgotten why he does it. No longer is he worried about pleasing his superiors. But this scrupulousness has caused him to push himself to the limit of a physical breakdown.

The pop psychologies and some religions promise that everything can be wonderful and that we can conquer all, and that we can achieve anything we can conceive and visualize strongly enough. But they are holding out a vision of human beings as perfectable, and that does not agree with the Bible, our experience, or the wisdom of the ages. Human beings can achieve remarkable things, but in God's eyes and by God's standards we are simply not perfectable, and the sooner we can relax with that truth, the more confident we will be.

It is a fine line we are drawing here: we want to avoid the arrogance of the person who has no conscience and feels no guilt. Grandiosity will not do. On the other hand, we want to avoid the self-contempt of the person whose life occupation is to apologize for existing.

PART
. . . . . .
FIVE

HOW LOVE
LEADS TO
SELF-CONFIDENCE

CONFIDENCE
· · · · · · · · · ·
CHAPTER ELEVEN

Nothing can make up for the absence
of someone whom we love,
and it would be wrong to try to find a substitute.
. . . It is nonsense to say that God fills the gap;
he does not fill it, but on the contrary,
he keeps it empty and so helps us to keep alive
our former communion with each other,
even at the cost of pain.

—DIETRICH BONHOEFFER

Building a Network of Supportive Relationships

SOMETIMES I ASK PEOPLE who come to see me if they're in any significant relationships.

"Are you in love, or do you have some good friendships?"

"No," the person often replies, "I'm not ready for that. I'm in counseling to get my self-image straightened out, then maybe I'll be ready to try some close relationships."

But that is like a middle-aged man postponing exercise until he is in shape. Identity and intimacy must occur hand in hand.

The view that a positive self-image must necessarily precede any positive relationships is one of the bromides of current self-help literature. Many books and weekend seminars emphasize that one must not depend on others for validation. It must all come from within, they say.

But it is a chicken-or-the-egg question. It is true that the greater our self-confidence, the better one will relate to others, yet healthy self-regard is not discovered on some desert island where we stare at our navels. We are defined in part by the people around us, and self-image is greatly enhanced by community. So one of the surest ways to improve confidence is to make sure you have a lot of love in your life, to take the necessary steps to construct a network of sustaining and nurturing relationships.

One way that love leads to self-confidence is when you:

▪▪▪

CULTIVATE PEOPLE
WHO HELP YOU GROW

▪▪▪

I have worked for an agonizingly long period with one woman in her thirties. But my own sense of anguish is nothing compared to hers, and I tell myself that I must persevere. Her situation is this: she lives in a large apartment complex in Los Angeles. In the morning she eats her breakfast alone, goes down to her parking garage, drives out onto the freeway, and parks in another underground garage beneath her office building. There she begins work in a little cubicle, working alone, with little interaction with the people whose cubicles surround her. She usually eats lunch alone, and at the end of the day, drives back to her apartment building and enters her empty apartment, where she almost never bothers to cook herself a hot meal, but eats while standing at the sink. And at 7:00 or 8:00 P.M. she lies down, hoping that she can fall asleep, "because," she says, "those 10 or 11 hours are the only relief I have from this horrible loneliness."

It is small wonder that this woman has had to be hospitalized three times and that she has been in and out of counseling all her adult life. The ancient rabbis were right when they said, "Anyone who goes too far alone goes mad."

It is easy to look at such a maladjusted person and dismiss her lack of friends as the result of an abrasive personality. There is some truth to that, of course. Though she desperately longs for companionship—and especially for romantic love—she does a lot of things to scare away anyone who gets close to her, and these rough edges to her personality need plenty of work. So it will not do, as some therapists have it, to concentrate on getting her self-image repaired, and then turn her loose to relate in the world. We must deal with her interpersonal problems one by one, and she and I must keep trying until some friendships begin to jell. I must be there to help her pick up the pieces when her relationships shatter, to help her figure out what she did wrong, and to take corrective measures to ensure more success next time.

The Need for Love

Human beings are made for love, and I find that many of my clients forget that. They scramble to shore up their self-images with various techniques, without giving sufficient attention to the source from which they will get help most readily—good friendships. They make all sorts of protests—that they're too busy, that they've learned to live without needing anyone, that they can't trust people, that they are really loners and prefer solitude. But it is all a smoke screen, and underneath lies a powerful aching to love and be loved.

Many people make the mistake of supposing that they will be happy only when they find the right man or the right woman to marry, neglecting the essential arena of friendship. Few of us are ready for a sexual relationship until we have learned to sustain a friendship. We do not have to marry to be happy, but we *do* have to have some love, and that can be found in the right type of friendships. The irony is that the persons who begin to relax in some solid friendships with people of the same sex—and stop worrying so much about meeting the man or woman of their dreams— begin to be much more attractive to the opposite sex. Friendship appears to be the best springboard to romance.

There is another reason to put more emphasis on friendship and less on romance: with the realities of divorce and death, most of us will have to spend at least some of our adult lives unmarried, so it is a poor strategy to put all our eggs in one basket. We could find ourselves entirely bereft of love when something happens to our mate. When a man says to me, "I don't need any other friends—my wife is my best friend," I do not applaud. He is putting too much pressure on his marriage, for there is no way any one person can meet all your emotional needs. To expect your mate to do so is to ask an impossible thing. Moreover, I fear for the man when, God forbid, he finds himself without his wife. Your mate should be your best friend, but not your only friend.

How does one go about building a circle of sustaining relationships? Most of my clients think the problem is in finding a place to meet new people. But the basic answer is not in meeting more people, it is in deepening the relationships we presently have. Many of us have acquaintances who could be promoted to friends, some friend who could be promoted to a good friend. It may seem easier to begin with someone new, but the best source of love is probably in your present circle of family and acquaintances.

The Importance of Family

Some of the women I counsel are in a panic because they have read the studies showing how slim their chances for marriage are if they have college degrees and are in their thirties. I've seen many older single women go through counseling who have suddenly found themselves getting married, so I am more optimistic about their chances than they are. Nevertheless, it is true that we cannot count on being in a nuclear family all our adult lives, and therefore it is important to make strong networks of support and nurture in many directions. One important direction is one's extended family—aunts and uncles, nieces, cousins, and grandparents.

A friend who is 45 years old tells me that when she goes back to visit her parents in Indiana it is always "a mixed bag." She makes connections with some relatives she would just as soon not see any more, and she usually has at least one blow-up with her parents. "But it's important to be around my family," she says. "I watch my grandmother's mannerisms, and my parents' ways, and say, 'So that's where I got that trait,' or '*that's* why I react this way.' Sometimes I say, 'I'm glad I have this characteristic, but that one I'm going to throw out.' And I always come back feeling that I know myself better and have a clearer idea, somehow, of who I am, where I came from, and where I want to go."

She is a wise woman. Some of us have disconnected ourselves from our pasts, moved thousands of miles away, and acted as if we were from outer space, when in fact we have roots—ancestors who have names and inheritable dispositions and identifiable physical characteristics. It is, as my friend says, "a mixed bag," but we need these connections with our heritage, for they help us to know that we're known by someone, that someone gave us a name, and that a clan still knows our name. Such connections make our identities more secure, for as John Dos Passos says, "A sense of continuity with the generations gone before can stretch like a lifeline across the scary present."

The Value of a Group

I learned long ago that my clients can sometimes get more from a month of group therapy than from a year of individual work. Part of the value of this is that the group can give you accurate feedback as to how you relate to others, because in such a group most of us eventually revert to our usual ways of connecting. And in an honest group people will tell you exactly how you come across, whereas most of society will not.

I would like to make a case for the enrichment and enhancement that such groups can give. AA provides splendid support for persons struggling with chemical dependency, and there are many other types of support groups for people with special interests and needs. Most churches have such groups. They vary in what they are called and how they are structured. For this purpose it is wise to select a group other than one gathered primarily for study (valuable as such groups are for other objectives). Instead, it should center on the feelings of the participants and build trust so that members of the group feel free to share personal concerns openly. Ideally, trust will build to a point where eventually you can tell each other anything.

Together with six other therapists and pastors, I belong to such a group that, for the lack of a better term, we call a covenant group. Since we live at some distance from each other, we meet only monthly, but that meeting is for a full, five-hour morning. In some ways it is the most important thing that happens to me all month. These men know the worst about me, and hold me accountable. When I am talking nonsense, or show signs of fatigue or superficiality, they say so. It is, along with my family, the place where people know me best, but at times I feel that they give me an even more accurate reading of my behavior and thoughts than even than my family can, for we are not so tied to specific roles. We are there to tell the truth, and to love each other. We do not walk away when one of us is exposing secret shadows. We continue to care what happens to each other and to display affection and regard for one another.

This group's life does not go on by itself. It takes work on each of our parts. It requires juggling our schedules so that we can be together. It requires dragging ourselves to the meeting when we must confess that we have not been able to stay with the resolves we promised last month. We are tempted to stay home at such times, but we have a pact that no matter how crowded our schedules, we show up. And we are always glad that we did, for though we may be tough on each other at times, there is no question that our brothers love us unconditionally, and this is of the utmost importance.

We also talk on the telephone between meetings. There are days when I get depressed and feel as if nobody loves me, and when one of the group's members spots that in my voice, he reassures me of my value. At such times they seem to like me better than I like myself.

I mention this support group to illustrate a very basic point: when we encircle ourselves with a few intimate friendships, we build for ourselves a pipeline that supplies a stream of sustaining reassurances that we exist, that we have worth. It does not happen without a great deal of effort, but it is worth every ounce of energy we expend.

I know of no single step one can take to enhance self-confidence that is as important as building a network of accepting, loving relationships. Sometimes the people who come for counseling are in such bad shape emotionally because they do not have enough love in their lives, and they are almost screaming, "Somebody please love me!" Progress comes when they are able to relax, stop begging for love, and begin loving. They look for someone for whom they can do a favor, someone to whom they can send a word of encouragement, someone whose shoulder they can put an arm around, and perhaps even begin to love. When we are "networking" merely for what we can get out of it, it usually backfires. But when we start finding others who need love and take the initiative in giving it to them, love seems to begin flowing back to us.

■ ■ ■ ■ ■ ■ ■ ■ ■ ■

CHAPTER TWELVE

*Demanding that people love us because we
cannot love ourselves is an iron-clad
guarantee of further rejection.*

—JUDITH VIORST

Coping
with Rejection

I'LL CALL HER BRENDA, but there are many wom-
en who could fit her description. The day I met Brenda
she had the appearance of a frightened bird. She was
strikingly beautiful. She was intelligent. She was well-
dressed. Yet as she talked about her loneliness and the
dreariness of her relationships, it was clear how miserable she was, and how desperately she longed for
someone who would give her love.

When I began counseling many years ago and first
worked with women like Brenda, I supposed that they
were overstating the situation. *Surely,* I would think
to myself, *a woman as good-looking as this must have
plenty of dates and many opportunities to fall in love.*
That I would jump to such conclusions shows how
naive I was about what is attractive to a man. Author
Alexandra Penny once asked hundreds of males to define the word *sexy.* The seven most frequent responses

were: "self-confident," "composed," "intelligent," "self-assured," "friendly," "feminine," and "at ease with her body." Beauty and having a voluptuous body were way down the list, and nobody said they wanted a woman who looked like a fashion model.

How was it that Brenda possessed so many outwardly beautiful attributes, but lacked the self-confidence to draw men? It came from her old memories of rejection. When Brenda was nine she grew five inches, and during junior high school she was always the tallest girl in the class. At 5'10" she stopped growing, and now, as a woman, her height sets off her good looks. But she cannot believe that, and she cannot remove from her mind the memories of school dances when all her friends would be chosen and she would be left alone. "Maybe you don't know what it's like, Dr. McGinnis," she said, "to be in a group and be the only one that's not chosen. It makes you feel like a piece of junk."

Here is a woman who still has inside her, like a stowaway, a painfully shy child, telling her to be careful lest she get into more situations where she will be rejected. And the result is that she is frightened and withdrawn. She seldom allows herself to be in places where she will meet men, and when she occasionally does have a date, she is cool and aloof. As soon as a relationship shows the least sign of trouble, she quickly bails out. It is easy to understand why—she has painful memories of rejection and will do almost anything to keep from feeling that pain again.

Or consider my friend Harry, whose wife left him four years ago, and who has withdrawn to his basement workshop. Harry was once a fairly outgoing, fun-loving guy who would enjoy a family picnic at the beach. But something snapped when Joan asked for a divorce. He does not date, he rarely visits his children (when he does he is very quiet), and when his friends call they usually get his answering machine.

In looking at Harry's reclusive life, some people might suppose that he has become hostile and bitter. But Harry is not bitter; he's simply depressed. He is convinced that if the woman who knew him best did not want to be married to him, who else would? And he thinks that his children and friends only call him because they feel sorry for him.

Although most of us have not been as scarred as Brenda or Harry, we have experienced rejection, and what is more, we are certain to experience it again. So how we cope with it is one of the most important factors in shaping our self-images and for our general success in life. A second way, then, that love leads to self-confidence is when you:

■■■■■■■■■■■■■■■■■■■■■■■■■■■■■■■■■■■■■■

REFUSE TO ALLOW REJECTION TO KEEP YOU FROM TAKING THE INITIATIVE WITH PEOPLE
■■■■■■■■■■■■■■■■■■■■■■■■■■■■■■■■■■■■■■

This is not only a cardinal rule for the development of relationships, but for almost every endeavor. I was speaking to a convention of marketing people some time ago when I met a manager who had been in sales all his life and had been very successful. Yet he did not appear to have the customary requirements for being a good salesman. His voice was high-pitched and he spoke rapidly, so that it was at times difficult to understand him. He didn't have the firm-handshake, look-you-in-the-eye approach. To the contrary, he seemed rather shy.

"How have you been so successful?" I asked.

"There's only one thing that makes someone good at sales," he said. "It's an ability to take rejection. It's the one quality you've got to have for success, and you'll never succeed without it."

What he says about selling holds true for love and friendship as well. I see many people who have been rejected. Perhaps they've had a love affair go sour, or they have been through a divorce, or there's been a rupture in their family. After going through these bad experiences, they became more and more wary that others would reject them, too. The result is a vicious circle: the more they suspect that rejection will come, the more often it comes. They withdraw, which others interpret as aloofness, and that turns people off, so the rejection comes with increasing velocity until eventually the person withdraws completely.

It is a mistake to assume that all self-doubt stems from bad experiences in childhood. Philip G. Zimbardo, professor of psychology at Stanford University, studied shy people for more than a decade and discovered that fully 40% of Americans claim to be of that disposition. The most surprising thing, Zimbardo discovered, was that fully 25% of those sufferers became shy *after* adolescence.

On the other hand, there are those who, as adults, have been badly treated by someone, and they come back even more self-possessed and more ready for love. At exactly 8:00 in the evening a woman in her sixties walks briskly from the wings to center stage of the Grace Rainey Rogers Auditorium at the New York Metropolitan Museum of Art. The hall is packed and the lecture series has been sold out for six months— as they always are when Rosamond Bernier gives her illustrated talks. The same is true when she appears at the National Gallery in Washington, D.C., the Minneapolis Institute of Arts, the Los Angeles County Museum of Art, and the many other well-known institutions that invite her back year after year. She says that she "doesn't even open her mouth these days" for less than $5000, and she receives many more invitations than she can accept. Calvin Trillin, writing about her in *The New Yorker,* said, "Rosamond Bernier has the lecturer's equivalent of perfect pitch. Forty or fifty times a year, she sails into her subject for the evening with a confidence and brio that rule out any possibility of boredom. . . . There is a quality of animation in her voice which keeps audiences alert. Life is great, the message reads, and even when it's not so great there are these people, artists and others, who make it seem better."

Has Rosamond Bernier always been this "up" and this fortunate? Far from it. The story of her misfortune is well known in art circles, and perhaps adds to her mystique: divorced by her husband, after 20 years of marriage, she was suddenly cut off from everything that mattered to her: an apartment in Paris, a country house and garden, and, worst of all, the art magazine which they had founded and edited together. Watching her now, it is hard to believe that Rosamond Bernier was emotionally incapacitated for nearly two years. But in 1969, Michael Mahoney, an art historian, heard Rosamond explaining Surrealism to a friend, and he was so impressed with her enthusiasm for the subject, her well-told anecdotes, and her perfect timing that, without telling her, he scheduled her for 14 lectures at Trinity College in Hartford. She was petrified at the prospect, but after the first lecture, it quickly became clear that she had a riveting stage presence. Her miraculous comeback into a new career had begun. She receives many letters from women who say they have drawn hope from her example. Her new marriage to John Russell, the chief art critic for the *The New York Times*, has been a happy one, and many women who have suffered similar misfortunes tell her that they admire her for taking charge of her own life in middle age, for not becoming a victim, and for not withdrawing.

Withdrawal—more than anything I know of—is the reason so many of my clients are lonely. What is the antidote? Or, to put it another way, how can you cope with rejection in such a way that it does not damage your self-image? Here are some strategies:

■ *Strategy 1: Expect rejection.* Some of us are taken off-guard when a relationship dries up or when someone turns on us and criticizes us, and because we did not expect it, the attack hits us harder than it should. Anyone who attempts anything significant in life is going to stumble—often. And like plants, some relationships die natural deaths. In other instances, we reach out to people and they spurn us.

Let us say that you meet a person who will perhaps make a good friend. Let us say that romance has nothing to do with it. He or she is simply a person you like. So you make an overture and reach out, but the other person shows little interest. Perhaps you try more than once—you suggest lunch, or you invite the person to your home, and each time the invitation is spurned. *This does not necessarily mean that there is anything wrong with you.* It may be that the other person's life circumstances are such that he or she would have responded very well a year earlier or a year later, but not now. Or it can be that closer examination shows that the two of you do not have much in common, and the other person sees that sooner than you do. Again, that does not mean that there is anything wrong with you.

▪ *Strategy 2: Consider the possibility that what you take to be rejection may not be rejection at all.* It is very sad to look back at lost opportunities for relationships and to realize that for want of going out on a limb, we lost the chance to give and receive love. Edward Dahlberg writes about how he longed to know the writer Theodore Dreiser, but he hesitated to interrupt this older, great man. "Should I telephone him," Dahlberg speculated, "he would surely hang up the receiver, and I would be mortally wounded." But eventually he took the risk, and Dreiser asked him to come right up to his apartment. Dahlberg gives this piercing account of the relationship that ensued:

My meetings with Dreiser continued, but I always was of the mind that I was ravaging his precious hours. Long after his death I read that, at the time we became acquainted, his closest friend had died and he hoped that Edward Dahlberg might take the lost friend's place. Time and again since then I have been bitten by the ever-hungry tooth of remorse. Good God, Theodore Dreiser needed me; and I, who have always been a beggar in any relationship, did not realize how desperately I required him!

▪ *Strategy 3: Recognize that some people reject everyone.* It is possible that the other person has been badly scarred and therefore does a lot of rejecting out of a desire for self-protection. In these situations you are not an isolated case: he or she is retaliating for some past wound by lashing out and hurting whenever possible. You are getting mail that should have been addressed to someone else. Again and again I see clients who are leaving behind them the carnage of many rejected people. Some are men who, because of their own insecurity and anger, set out to make women fall in love, and then, as soon as they have done so, drop them and move on. If a woman happens to meet two or three such men in a row, it would be quite easy for her to conclude that there is some basic flaw in her, when in fact she has simply met a string of men who are covertly malicious.

▪ *Strategy 4: Try to learn from the rejection.* If you keep coming up to bat and do not worry about the times you strike out, you will eventually hit a home run. But that does not mean that you should ignore the lessons of your strike-outs. It could be that you are unwittingly doing some things that cause some of the rejection, and it would be foolish not to find out what they are. Once you have the facts before you, you can decide what, if anything, you wish to change. Perhaps you will want to ask the person, or perhaps ask other friends. To say to someone, "I seem to be messing up a lot of my friendships. What do you think it is that's causing this?" makes a person very vulnerable, but, if you have the courage for it, you might learn a great deal.

■ *Strategy 5: Allow yourself the right to get angry.* From some rejections you need to discover what your mistake was and apologize. In other instances you need to get angry. If that sounds excessive, I would like to introduce you to Joan, whose husband Stewart was having an affair. To make matters worse, the other woman was her best friend. How did Joan react? After the shock of discovery and crying and screaming for a night, Joan persuaded herself that it was all *her* fault. She forced herself to call her friend to say that she understood how these things could happen, and that she hoped they could still be friends. The more she thought about it, she had failed her husband in so many ways. She had never given him this and she had never understood that. She had failed to meet his needs or keep up with the ironing. After several weeks of beating up on herself, *she* was the one to apologize.

"I want you to forgive me," she said, "for making you so miserable and forcing you into an affair."

Stewart told her he'd think about it.

By the time he had finished thinking about it, Joan was suicidally depressed. What she should have been was angry.

■ *Strategy 6: Keep trying until you connect.* The people who tuck their heads down and keep trying new relationships are eventually going to meet others with whom the chemistry works. Criticism comes to everyone. In fact, the more you're admired by some, and the more successful you become, the more visible a target you are for critics. So don't withdraw just because you've been rejected. Determine that you're going to keep going through as many rejections as are necessary until you find the love you need.

I am a psychotherapist in a huge metropolitan area, and I'm often frustrated that so many clients whom I come to know as wonderful but lonely people do not meet each other. It is simply unnecessary for so many people to be sitting at home wishing someone would walk into their lives. If they could learn to be less sensitive about occasional short circuits and to swallow hard and try again when they fail, they could develop the kind of relationships they need.

The root of the matter, if we want a stable world,
is a simple and old-fashioned thing,
a thing that I am almost ashamed to mention,
for fear of the derisive smiles
with which wise cynics will greet my words.
The thing I mean is love, Christian love.

—BERTRAND RUSSELL

Self-Confidence without Self-Worship

WE MUST NOW DEAL WITH A PROBLEM against which we have bumped several times: how to avoid, in the process of gaining self-confidence, the sin of pride.

Joan Kennedy assessed herself for a *Ladies' Home Journal* interviewer some time ago:

I have talent. I know I'm smart. I got straight A's in graduate school. I've still got my looks. I know I've got all these terrific things going for me. I mean, my God, you are talking to, I think, one of the most fascinating women in this country.

171

Such self-praise and inflated egoism is so common-place that it may well be on its way to becoming standard talk. Yet the ostentatious braggart always looks ridiculous, fraudulent, or worse, for we know intuitively what the Bible says repeatedly: our tendency to self-idolatry eventually leads to self-destruction.

The Antidote to Narcissism

How, then, can we gain self-confidence without self-worship? The solution lies in Jesus' two-part reply to a Pharisee's question about which commandment was the greatest:

> "Love the Lord your God with all your heart and with all your soul and with all your mind." This is the first and greatest commandment. And the second is like it: "Love your neighbor as yourself" (Matt. 22:37-39).

This is not only a brilliantly succinct theological summary; it may also be the most important psychological remark ever made, elegant in its simplicity. There are to be two anchors to our self-assurance: worship and compassion.

The Upward Look

On the first point, Jesus was not merely saying that we should go to church regularly. He urged that we get passionately caught up in the grandeur of God: "Love the Lord your God with all your heart and with all your soul and with all your mind." This depicts a person whose many parts have become unified in a joyous and passionate commitment.

The *Book of Common Prayer* says we are to "give thanks to God for His Glory," because we owe God gratitude for who he is rather than for any particular benefit God has conferred on us. Such transcendence of ourselves in worship gets us beyond the temptation to be unduly preoccupied with ourselves. Yet there is no question about such a person becoming a wimp—passionate believers are not weak, they are very, very strong.

The Nature of Christian Humility

This question of personal strength is an important one, for some Christians seem to think that being properly humble is being a Mr. Milquetoast who is always telling you he is nobody. Leading the devout life does not mean that we must walk about with our eyes lowered, regularly apologizing, criticizing ourselves, and putting ourselves down: "I'm no good at names," "I'm terribly sorry to bother you," "I can never seem to get anywhere on time," "I'm very poor at this."

Such self-depreciation is nowhere advocated in the Bible and is psychologically dangerous, for if allowed to become a habit, it can become predictive: when we talk that way long enough, we can indeed find ourselves forgetting people's names, becoming clumsier or less successful. Such self-denigration ought to be removed from our vocabularies, and we should say nothing about ourselves that we do not wish to become true.

For some, self-criticism is almost a reflex action, as if the person were attempting to find a way to sound properly modest. But as C. S. Lewis said, Christian humility is not the fawning, self-deprecating way of a woman who, when asked to play the piano at a meeting says, "Oh, no, I don't play well, I'm sure there are others who could do it better than I," when she knows very well that she is the best pianist in the group. That, says Lewis, is not humility, but false modesty. Humility is recognizing that you are a good pianist and taking pleasure in it. But you do not get a big head about it, because you know it is a gift from God. Worship is the anchor that keeps confidence from becoming pride.

I have been saying in these chapters that we ought to think very highly of ourselves, since we are God's creation, wondrously made in God's image. Moreover, we have the assurance that God loves us, knows our names, cares for our welfare, and has laid plans for us to live forever with him. To acknowledge these facts about ourselves is not to become proud and arrogant; quite to the contrary, keeping everything within this perspective would make vanity absurd.

I once took a business trip with a building contractor, with whom I shared a hotel room. He is a very persuasive and successful executive who commands respect everywhere he goes. In part, he gets this respect because of his size: he is 6′ 4″, powerfully built, with hands the size of catchers' mitts. But he also commands respect because of the dignity and self-assurance of his demeanor—when people meet him they seem to recognize that here is a person in possession of himself.

The first evening of our trip, I had a glimpse into the source of that power. I had turned on the lamp on my nightstand, crawled into bed, and propped up my magazine to begin reading. It is, I suppose, the way I have gone to bed for 30 years.

But my friend had a different ritual. He turned on his lamp, then knelt beside his bed to silently say his prayers. It is difficult to describe what I felt when I glanced over and saw that he was praying. The novelist James Joyce might have called it an epiphany—one of those moments of ordinary life when everything around you is illuminated.

The Outward Look

Worship is a counterweight to pride. Now we must look at its counterpoint, which is a life of compassion. We are to love our neighbor as ourselves. Such love encompasses the close relationships with family and friends discussed in the previous chapter, but when Christ commanded us to love our neighbor, he meant far more than networking. For when the lawyer asked for an elaboration on who his neighbor was, Jesus went on to tell the story of the good Samaritan. We are to love those who are poor and who are strangers to us.

"The antidote to boredom is not distraction but service," writes John Gardner, founder of Common Cause, and we can have great self-confidence without having it turn into pride, so long as we are always looking for places to serve and to love. When author Evelyn Underhill sought out theologian Friedrich von Hügel as a spiritual mentor, he suggested, among other things, that she turn away from her erudite studies and spend two afternoons a week among poor persons in the slums of London. It is the sort of balance all of us need—to move from the cloister to the grimy arena of those who suffer. The self-obsession of our popular culture is quite different in its determination to "have it all," to find happiness by forgetting about family, future generations, and social obligations. It is me, me, me.

Henri Nouwen, the Roman Catholic priest many of us admire for his cogent books on theology and psychology, made a statement more important than anything in his books when he left his teaching post at Harvard in August 1985 and went to France to live and work in a small colony for mentally retarded persons. Some years before, he had met Jean Vanier, the founder of l'Arche—a network of communities for emotionally handicapped people. The house at Trosly-Breuil, a little village outside of Paris, began in 1964 when Jean Vanier decided to invite Raphael and Philippe, who for many years had lived in a mental institution and had no family or friends, to form a small foyer (home) with him. It was an irreversible decision. He knew he could never send these two men back to where they had come from.

He called his first foyer "l'Arche," the French word for "the ark," thus indicating that he wanted his home to be like Noah's ark, a refuge for fearful people. Jean did not think about starting a movement or a large organization. He simply began caring for two people who could not manage without help. But soon, people arrived from different countries to offer assistance. They were people like Nouwen, a refugee from the intellectual world of Harvard Divinity School, who decided he would rather spend his days serving and bathing and cooking for people in need.

Most of us are not free to leave everything and move into a home for retarded persons. Sometimes Christian service is not some grand act of heroism, it is a small act of kindness. Even toward strangers we can offer a balm in Gilead. A friend who is a salesman says that he has two goals for each day: (1) he tries to do something he does not like to do, and (2) he tries to go out of his way to do something for somebody for which he knows he will not be recognized.

A reporter once asked Mother Teresa how she measured the success and failure of her work. Her reply was that she did not think God used categories like success and failure. The measurement instead was this: "How much have you loved?"

It would be interesting to know what sort of self-regard people like Mother Teresa and Henri Nouwen—who seem to love so well—carry around with them. I suspect that they do not think much about the matter. My guess is that they arise in the morning with zest because they are caught up in lives of worship and service. There is so much to do that they do not have time to take their emotional pulse and ask, "Am I happy today?" They are too busy loving.

At times it seems strange that Jesus told us we would find ourselves by losing ourselves. We have some inkling of what that means when we see people such as Father Nouwen, my friend the salesman, and Mother Teresa. Each of the three is quite strong-willed, but their strong wills do not lead to inflated egos, because they devote themselves to love of God and love of their neighbors.

It is the love of God that provides the foundation of our identities, and because we are then given such a peaceful center—such a point of reference that keeps us mentally sound—we are able to turn and give ourselves to others. The paradox is that such giving of ourselves to our neighbors does not threaten our self-image, but rather reinforces it. The amazing thing about love, Rollo May says, is that it is the best way to get to know ourselves. Self-confidence, like happiness, is slippery when we set out to grab it for its own sake. Usually it comes rather as a by-product. We lose ourselves in service, and suddenly one day we awake to realize that we are confident and rather happy.

■■■■■

What began as a book about the various ways we perceive ourselves now turns out to be a book about love, for it is from loving and being loved that confidence best emerges, and ultimately it is divine love that sets this all in perspective.

Until this closing chapter I have avoided the phrase "self-love," because I am uncomfortable with the ring of those words. They sound too much like a conceited person we describe as being "terribly in love with himself." Yet it was self-love that was implied when Jesus commanded us to love our neighbors as ourselves. If we *are* to love ourselves, clearly it is not to be with the pride against which wise writers have inveighed again and again. Rather, it is to be the sort of relationship we have with our most cherished friends: we accept them, faults and all, and we are devoted to their best interests. We have made a commitment to them, and out of that commitment we care for them and nurture them. It should be the same in our relationship to ourselves.

Or to use a better illustration, we are to love ourselves as God loves us: God is not overly impressed with us—he knows our flaws. But we are God's children, and God is benevolently interested in our welfare. So if we are to call it "self-love," we must see it as this relaxed appreciation and healthy regard for the beloved.

The three loves—love of God, self, and neighbor—are closely bound together. All are subsumed in the first commandment—we are to love the Lord our God with heart, soul, and mind. Because of this secure relationship we are able to have a healthy regard both for ourselves and for one another—we will love our neighbors as ourselves.

It is a curious thing how love and laughter go together. When you first fall in love with someone, you seem to find so many things funny, and you easily collapse into each other's arms over a hilarious episode. One of the marks of a gathering of good friends is the hearty laughter that breaks out. And the saving grace of healthy self-confidence is its capacity to be as amused by one's own foibles as by those of others.

A few years ago I appeared as part of a discussion panel on one of the religious television networks. I was nervous about what I was going to say, and a little concerned about what the audience would think of me.

When I speak to groups, I talk freely about my Christian faith, but I don't always use traditional, "spiritual" vocabulary. And besides, I was worried about how I looked. I was 30 pounds overweight, and my coat kept tugging at its button.

Then a man joined us who was much fatter than I, who laughed at the drop of a hat, and who was the star of the show. He had been successful at four or five different occupations and was now semiretired. On television he did not try to hide his stomach—he sat on the edge of his chair, waved his arms, and let his coat fly open and his tie go where it would. He laughed, he groaned, he roared, and his eyes shone with surprise and delight. He was relaxed, confident, and he did not pretend to be anything more than what he was.

In evangelical circles, there is a great deal of talk about "being constantly in prayer" and having regular family devotions. But he told the world that he did not follow the practice. "Frankly," he said to the camera, "Harriet and I have tried all kinds of ways of having Bible study and prayer and it just doesn't work for us. I'm not particularly proud of this, but I'm just telling you the way it is at our house. The only time we pray together is when we go to bed. We cuddle into each others' arms and say a prayer and then we just lie there and hold each other, and that makes everything right."

He was equally candid about the spectacular flops of his life. He had been fired from a top executive position. "They told me that they would announce that I had resigned so it wouldn't look so bad, but they wanted me to clear out my desk on Sunday so there would be no questions asked. I had never been fired from a job in my life."

"Was that traumatic for you?" asked the interviewer.

"Traumatic?" he exclaimed. "I went home and went to bed and pulled the blanket over my face for two days. But my wife loved me. She knew I'd done some things wrong and she had been waiting. She is a spiritual woman, and she loved me back into wholeness."

As I watched him talk, I realized how little our bodily configuration has to do with our attractiveness. Millions of American women were watching this overweight fellow talk and probably would have given anything to have a husband like him. Rather than some ascetic, self-contained, cold person who is unsure of himself, we prefer to be around a relaxed person such as this, who knows how to laugh and to love.

This man, who became my friend, is a good example of healthy self-love. He does not take himself too seriously, he is open about his shortcomings, and he laughs at himself readily. Yet there is a dignity about him also. His self-worth comes from being a child of God, and he does not squander his life—he leads a life that includes service to others, and he cares passionately for certain people who come across his path. Success and failure seem to come and go, but he does not take that too seriously either, for it is enough to serve God, to do the best he can with what he has, and to catch joy when it comes.

Immanuel Kant, the great philosopher, said that if there is any science we badly need, it is one that will tell us "how to occupy properly that place in creation that is assigned to man." My friend seems to have found his place better than some of us who try to be philosophers and psychologists. He has found the proper middle ground between self-contempt and self-worship.

That middle ground is a comfortable place, where we can walk purposefully and assuredly, and yet where we can laugh at our foibles when our companions tell us we are wrong. It is a place where we can be at ease with both our gifts and our shortcomings, our vast potential and our penchant for sin, aware that on the one hand we are dust and on the other that we are "a little less than God, crowned with glory and honor." We are at ease with both sides because we know that both sides are in the hands of God.

Notes

Scripture quotations unless otherwise noted are from the Holy Bible: New International Version. Copyright 1978 by the New York International Bible Society. Used by permission of Zondervan Bible Publishers.

p. 30   Material from "Peanuts" by Charles Schultz reprinted by permission of United Feature Syndicate, Inc.

p. 37   Quotations from *The Disowned Self* by Nathaniel Branden (New York: Bantam, 1971), p. 99, used by permission of Nathaniel Branden, Ph.D.

p. 41   The material from *Our Many Selves* by Elizabeth O'Connor, p. xxi, is copyright © 1971 by Elizabeth O'Connor. Published by Harper and Row, Publishers, Inc.

pp. 51-56   Material adapted from *Type A Behavior and Your Heart* by Meyer Friedman and Ray H. Rosenman (New York: Ballantine/ Fawcett, 1981), © 1981 Fawcett Crest.

pp. 57-58   The friar's quotation is from *When I Relax, I Feel Guilty* by Tim Hansel (Elgin, Ill.: David C. Cook, 1979), pp. 44-45, © 1979. Used with permission by David C. Cook Publishing Company.

p. 61   Material adapted from Srully Blotnick is from *Getting Rich Your Own Way* (New York: Doubleday, 1980).

pp. 65-66   The story of Helen Yglesias is from *Late Bloomers* by Carol Colman and Michael A. Perelman (New York: Macmillan, 1985), pp. 47-48, 50-51. Copyright © 1985 Carol Colman and Michael A. Perelman. Used by permission of Macmillan Publishing Company.

CONFIDENCE

∎

pp. 66-67   The list of individuals and their achievements is from *The Book of Ages* by Desmond Morris (New York: Viking, 1983), as reprinted in "Your Age Is What *You* Make It," *Reader's Digest,* December 1984, p. 27.

p. 73   Quotations from *Cognitive Behavior Modification* by Donald H. Meichenbaum (New York: Plenum, 1977), p. 32, are used by permission of Plenum Publishing Corporation and Donald H. Meichenbaum.

pp. 82-83   Material adapted from *Peak Performance* by Charles Garfield (Los Angeles: Jeremy P. Tarcher, 1984), pp. 17-19, is reprinted with permission of Dr. Charles P. Garfield.

p. 89   Material about Thomas I. Fatjo Jr. is from *With No Fear of Failure* by Keith Miller and Thomas I. Fatjo Jr. (New York: Berkeley Publishing, 1984).

pp. 94-95   Material from "Strictly Personal" by Sydney J. Harris is copyright © 1960 Field Enterprises, Field Newspaper Syndicate. Used by permission of North American Syndicate, Inc.

pp. 96-97   Material by Neil Clark Warren is used by permission of Neil Clark Warren.

pp. 97-98   The Risë Stevens material is excerpted from "The Best Advice I Ever Had" by Risë Stevens, *Reader's Digest,* July 1955. Reprinted with permission.

p. 99   Material from "The More Sorrowful Sex" by Maggie Scarf, *Psychology Today,* April 1979, is reprinted with permission from *Psychology Today Magazine,* copyright © 1979 (APA).

pp. 102-103   The excerpts about Renoir are from *Renoir, My Father* by Jean Renoir, translated by Randolph and Dorothy Weaver (Boston: Little, Brown, 1962), pp. 449, 456-458.

Notes

■

p. 106   Quotations excerpted from *Time to Remember* by Rose Kennedy (New York: Doubleday, 1974), p. 188, are copyright © 1974 by Joseph P. Kennedy Jr. Foundation. Reprinted with permission of Doubleday and Company, Inc.

pp. 107-108   The Marlo Thomas material is from "Marlo Thomas: My Life Gets Better All the Time," *McCalls*, August 1978, p. 86. Used by permission.

pp. 112   The line from T. S. Eliot is from *The Cocktail Party* by T. S. Eliot, copyright 1950 by T. S. Eliot; renewed 1978 by Esme Valerie Eliot. Reprinted by permission of Harcourt Brace Jovanovich, Inc.

pp. 115-117   The Harold Bloomfield material is from the book *Making Peace with Your Parents* by Harold H. Bloomfield, M.D., published by Ballantine Books, © 1983 Bloomfield Productions.

pp. 123-124   Quotations from Cynthia Gorney are from "If You Hate Your Knobby Knees, Fat Thighs, Big Feet, or Small Breasts, Don't Worry. You May Never Love Your Imperfections, but You Can Live Happily with Them—Honest!" by Cynthia Gorney, *Seventeen*, August 1980.

pp. 126-127   Gail MacDonald quotations are from *High Call, High Privilege* by Gail MacDonald (Wheaton: Tyndale, 1981), pp. 54-55, 67, © 1981 Tyndale House Publishers, Inc. Used by permission.

pp. 129-130   The Ann Landers material is reprinted with permission of Ann Landers, Los Angeles Times Syndicate, as printed in "Sex, Why Women Feel Shortchanged," *Family Circle*, June 11, 1985.

pp. 136-137   The Willard Gaylin material is adapted from *Feelings: Our Vital Signs* by Willard Gaylin, M.D. (New York: Harper and Row, 1979), pp. 40-42, copyright © 1979 by Willard Gaylin. Harper and Row Publishers, Inc.

CONFIDENCE

.

pp. 138-139   The Judith Viorst quotation is from *Necessary Losses* by Judith Viorst (New York: Simon and Schuster, 1986), p. 132. Used by permission.

pp. 146-147   The Norman Vincent Peale quotations are from *Positive Imaging* by Norman Vincent Peale (Old Tappan, N.J.: Revell, 1982), copyright © 1982 by Norman Vincent Peale. Published by Fleming H. Revell Company. Used by permission.

pp. 167-168   The Theodore Dreiser and Edward Dahlberg material is from *Search for Silence* by Elizabeth O'-Connor (San Diego: LuraMedia, 1986), p. 22, copyright 1986 LuraMedia, San Diego, California. Reprinted by permission.

Index of Names